Appearance and Inference

Appearance and Inference

Edward Allbless

Copyright © 2018 Edward Allbless

The moral right of the author has been asserted.

Apart from any fair dealing for the purposes of research or private study, or criticism or review, as permitted under the Copyright, Designs and Patents Act 1988, this publication may only be reproduced, stored or transmitted, in any form or by any means, with the prior permission in writing of the publishers, or in the case of reprographic reproduction in accordance with the terms of licences issued by the Copyright Licensing Agency. Enquiries concerning reproduction outside those terms should be sent to the publishers.

Matador
9 Priory Business Park,
Wistow Road, Kibworth Beauchamp,
Leicestershire. LE8 0RX
Tel: 0116 279 2299
Email: books@troubador.co.uk
Web: www.troubador.co.uk/matador
Twitter: @matadorbooks

ISBN 978 1789014 556

British Library Cataloguing in Publication Data.
A catalogue record for this book is available from the British Library.

Printed on FSC accredited paper
Printed and bound in Great Britain by 4edge Limited
Typeset in 11pt Adobe Garamond Pro by Troubador Publishing Ltd, Leicester, UK

Matador is an imprint of Troubador Publishing Ltd

This book is dedicated to my late sister, Sheroo Hartley, without whose guidance I would be a lost soul.

Introduction

Inference is a powerful tool because it generally plays a central role in the activity of thinking. That said, inference as an activity is something of a 'science', albeit a 'science' which is not universally understood. As a consequence it is capable of misuse. Nor are its various rules always correctly applied, and we are often guilty of inferring too much, or inferring something which is qualitatively different from the premises we have started with.

Certain kinds of inference, or inferences drawn from certain kinds of phenomena or certain kinds of premise, are misleading or incorrect. And not every inference is an inference validly drawn.

Invalid inferences are the result of one of two errors: firstly, an error resulting from an incorrect premise, or a premise whose meaning is uncertain or unclear; or secondly, an error which is the consequence of the incorrect application of the rules of inference.

The purpose of this short book is to consider a number of these types of error.

PART I

The Application of Logic

On the Meaning of Freedom of Will

Just as it is apparently impossible to incontrovertibly decide whether or not a god exists – because we define the word in such a way as to render the concept incapable of ordinary proof – it is not possible to incontrovertibly decide whether or not man has freedom of will. Firstly, we are unsure just how to construe 'will'; and secondly, we cannot agree with one another on a comprehensible concept of freedom. If an exercise of will were the same as to choose between more than one eventuality, and freedom were the same as making that choice in an 'unfettered' manner (in short, being capable of choosing either alternative), then I would ask why it is so crucial that we decide that issue at all. It seems clear that at least *some* of our actions or choices are made 'consciously', so to speak, in so far as we appear to be 'aware' of having considered and subsequently made that choice; and that should suffice. That we are aware of the decision we have taken and, in some instances, we have ascribed a reason for making that decision, and perhaps also a reason as to why we had not elected to take an alternative decision, is sufficient to constitute an action that is in some sense 'free'. Of course, it is possible that in some instances we may be deluding ourselves as to the reason we have given for our action. It is possible that the reason given is not *in fact* the reason why we have acted thus, but it is arguable that in at least some cases, we are capable of providing what appears to be a plausible, if not *the* reason, why we have chosen one option rather than another.

I chose to study philosophy at Oxford, and it is arguable that that choice was made 'freely', so to speak, in so far as I did not do so under duress, or as a consequence of the advice or prompting of another.

One might argue that something in my nature, or rather my nature itself (by which we mean, probably, no less than the sum of qualities or properties which one conceives I possess, which is itself a presumption – for how is one to ascertain that each individual is a composite of qualities in that sense?) has not merely enabled me, but indeed caused me, in the sense that I am obligated, so to speak (at least in a mechanistic sense, rather than in an ethical sense), to make that choice. In the circumstances, let us say, I could not have made any other choice.

That is a curious argument, for by that argument a 'free' choice is one which would appear to have no antecedents whatsoever, and would appear to be wholly arbitrary. Though it is just possible to conceive of circumstances in which an action might be wholly arbitrary, I cannot see the value (humankind being such as it is) in making a wholly arbitrary decision; and therefore, if free will comprises an action which has no antecedents and to that degree is entirely unpredictable, though it may well exist, such freedom of will is valueless.

Indeed, I suggest that the only form of free will which *is* of value (humankind being such as it is) must comprise an action which is entirely predictable in the light of the particular nature of the *actor*. In addition to that, in order to make a free choice, as it were, it has to be physically (and notionally) possible for that individual to make any one of the alternative choices available to him.

Perhaps I chose the study of philosophy because as a younger man, the bigger picture, so to speak, was an area of human study that fascinated me. This was an area of study which so closely coincided with my own thoughts and the manner in which I myself often thought, that I felt, let us say, 'compelled', better still 'driven', to choose that area of study. To the extent that that choice was made, to the best of my belief and (self-) knowledge, for a reason of which I appeared to be aware and which I had thought through, as it were, is an indication that that choice was mine, and to that degree, that it was freely made.

If, on the contrary, I had chosen to take up lawn tennis as an 'occupation' (assuming that I had needed one at all, to see me through the days), that might well have been entirely unpredictable, both by observers outwith me as well as by myself, upon reflection; but given the qualities which I possess, and my singular inability to excel at anything sporting, so to speak, that choice would have been (one might say) wholly 'out of character', and doomed to failure!

As a consequence, I suggest that my choice of

philosophy as a course of serious study was not only entirely 'in character', given my particular qualities, but was a key factor in my personal growth. That I might have considered that choice to be the most suitable in the circumstances, such that I declined to choose otherwise, does not, I suggest, make that choice any the less free, because freedom of choice cannot possibly comprise the power to make choices which are wholly without antecedents.

[In any event, like many of the words we use in everyday parlance, the word 'freedom' begins its existence, so to speak, not as a concept but as an impression (often a vague impression), which some of us then set about giving 'conceptual form'. Personally, I think that is an entirely back-to-front exercise! Where is the wisdom in forming an impression, however strong that impression may be, and only after the fact, trying to give that impression conceptual form? That would be as peculiar as coining a name and then looking for a suitable owner for it. If some time ago we coined the word 'freedom' but try as we might, we are unable to say what that could mean, save in some rather vague sense, then where is the wisdom in forcing a definition? If it cannot be defined, let us admit that to one another; and if notwithstanding we doggedly continue to use the word, let us also admit to ourselves that we use the word merely to describe an impression, possibly with no universally acceptable associated meaning.]

On Appearance and Inference

To infer something is to apply certain agreed rules of logic to the form of a statement or proposition.

Take the following example of an application of these rules:

- If Sam was born in Canada, then he is a Canadian
- Sam was not born in Canada
- Sam is not a Canadian

This may appear to be a valid form of argument, but I suggest that it is troublesome, and in practice can lead to an incorrect inference. It may be true that Sam was not born in Canada. But he may have acquired Canadian citizenship through a process of naturalization, and so he may indeed be a Canadian! Clearly, we are missing potentially a number of other steps or premises. For example,

- One means of acquiring Canadian citizenship is through the process of naturalization;

- Sam has applied for Canadian citizenship by submitting an application for naturalization;
- Sam's application was successful;
- Sam is a Canadian.

Inference is a tool we routinely use in most, if not all, forms of enquiry. But our inferences can sometimes lead us to assume too much.

We draw inferences when we analyze our various experiences. But attempting an analysis of the nature of knowledge is fraught with difficulty, and in doing so we rely on a range of types of assumption or presumption. For example, it is presumed that certain 'qualities' exist, in the sense that such qualities *are*; but that there also exists something else to which these qualities 'belong', or something which 'perceives' these qualities, is not a necessary or logical conclusion therefrom; and yet we draw that conclusion fearlessly. Nor is *cogito ergo sum* so obviously the case, but of course, philosophers since Descartes have recognised this.

Characterising 'red' as a sensation and 'grunt' as a sound is itself illegitimate, and leads to the illegitimate inference that each *belongs* to something. If we start with the premise 'I think', we are inevitably led to 'I am'. What I am concerned with, in this instance, is akin to an inappropriate use of *modus ponendo ponens*.

Though it is possible to say that there exists 'red' or 'grunt', it is not necessary, as an inference or a logical conclusion therefrom, to conclude that there also exists something which has (in some sense as though emanating or deriving from, or necessarily associated with) 'red' or 'grunt', or that 'red' and 'grunt' are qualities.

It is therefore illegitimate to conclude that because p (let us suppose that p is either equivalent to or the same as our example of sensation; or alternatively, that it has linguistic or symbolical form, say a word, or a series of words), therefore there 'exists' (in the same sense, let us suppose, as we use that word to refer to the sensation itself) a subject who thinks p, or to whom that thought 'belongs' (in the sense that that thought emanates or derives *from* that subject).

Legitimately, there *is* no necessary conclusion, in the sense that that conclusion is *logically* (or even metaphysically) necessary, or follows from the supposed existence of 'red' or 'grunt'.

Our use of language to describe that perception can indeed lead us to an illegitimate conclusion. What appears comparatively less difficult to demonstrate is 'red'; but to attempt to demonstrate that 'I [sense] red' or '*I* [sense] red' is more problematical, as it is not (even linguistically) a logically necessary conclusion, or associated (again, in some logical sense) with 'red'. It is also illegitimate to conclude from 'red', that that 'red' in some manner 'belongs' to something.

It is in fact perfectly legitimate that 'red' is the totality, and it is unnecessary to infer that either red is perceived, or that it is merely a quality possessed by something; unless one takes the illegitimate step that, because 'red', and on the basis or with the understanding that 'red' is *necessarily* a 'perception', therefore 'red' must by necessity be perceived, and as a consequence, perceived *by* a percipient. It would then be a further unnecessary step to conclude that *because* 'red', there must be *something* which is 'red'.

-2-

The question 'how do you know that you have toothache?' (setting aside for a moment the issues arising from solipsism) is not a nonsensical question, if one considers the question in the context of possible hallucination or self-delusion. To that extent, it is indeed necessary and possible to have or conduct (at least limited) verification for 'I have' statements, such as 'I have toothache', and also to give the statement some meaning.

An associated question is, how do we ascertain whether an experience is delusional? In short, how do we distinguish between that which is delusional and that which is factual? Further, are only certain kinds of experience necessarily factual? Can a mystical experience ever be construed as containing factual content, or as itself comprising a fact?

Statements of fact or delusion give rise to other difficulties. Surely it is not possible to distinguish between factual and delusional statements *per se*, at least in as far as such statements comply with the rules of linguistic form. To that extent, the statement 'I saw a man standing before me' can be either delusional or factual, and it is not the form of the statement itself which enables us to distinguish one from the other. Indeed, in one sense at least, the verificationists were correct in their analysis of language. If we wish to distinguish between true and false statements, or as I have put it, factual and delusional statements, we would have to evaluate or discover the correspondence between the statement as a proposition and a certain state of affairs. The state of affairs is itself an assumption which is itself incapable of verification, but the truth of it may be supported by 'evidence', in the form of other assumptions of a similar kind. Accordingly, 'I saw a man standing before me' asserts at minimum as follows: that there is an observer; and that an object, in this case in the form of a man, was located in a certain spatial relationship with that observer. If it can be incontrovertibly shown that no such man stood before our observer, or that what the observer took to be a man was in fact a tree, then the observer's statement is shown to be delusional or incorrect. But given that it cannot incontrovertibly be shown that no such man exists, we can only present evidence to show that the assumption of the man's existence is difficult to sustain.

If statements such as that are to make 'sense', then we must also necessarily make sense or be capable of making sense of the components of that statement: the words 'I', 'I saw', 'a man', 'standing', 'before', 'before me', and 'me'. If any one or more of these components is meaningless, or if their meaning is difficult to ascertain, the statement itself is on shaky ground and may not readily convey meaning.

Another example. It is conceivable that the question 'how do you know that you have toothache?' is likewise capable of a degree of confirmation, if it is possible for a third party to show that I cannot possibly have toothache, because I do not in fact have teeth in that part of my mouth which aches, or at all! That does not, however, necessarily disprove the existence of the ache itself. All one can legitimately assert is that the ache is not a *tooth*ache. The issue therefore is an issue of mere semantics.

We could easily envisage a more comprehensible example. We have heard of instances where an individual who has had to have a limb amputated continues (on occasion) to feel sensation in what appears to him or her to be that very limb. If one were to ask 'how do you know that you have an ache in your right arm?', the question would clearly have some sense, some capacity for confirmation, if in fact the subject in question had had his right arm removed, and an observer would easily be able to verify the truth or falsehood of the statement 'I have an ache in my [amputated] right arm'. Again, as with the toothache, we have demonstrated that 'I have an ache in my right arm' is false, but we cannot therefore necessarily negate or confirm the truth of 'I have an ache'.

Accordingly, though the form of the proposition 'I have a toothache' is not in itself in issue, whether that proposition bears a direct relationship with what we loosely call 'fact' is indeed, or can be, in issue. As a consequence, one needs to look further than merely at the linguistic form of a proposition in order to determine its veracity. Assuming that we have reason to believe in a factual world, outwith an observer, a proposition must also necessarily bear a relationship with that factual world. And *there* lies the challenge!

So much for statements of purported fact. It is much more difficult to try to ascribe meaning to a more abstract statement such as 'I have the freedom to choose between two alternatives'. I will deal with the truth values of abstract statements in a subsequent section of this book.

-3-

In language there are no primary forms or 'simples'. Even names or designates can be further analysed, and defined, and in some cases may not enable us to identify the object they are purportedly naming.

Take the compound form 'the tree is ten feet tall'. The word closest in kind to a simple, in this communication, is 'tree' (perhaps because it designates an apparently discrete phenomenon which we call an 'object'). But that too, in the absence of the simple act of pointing, can be further defined as, say, organic form belonging to the plant kingdom having a woody bark, or somesuch. Indeed, the more one describes or attempts to define the 'simple', the more complex and multi-faceted becomes each component of that further description. Plant kingdom, woody, bark, and so on, *ad infinitum*; or at least potentially so. Indeed, in order to use the word 'tree' correctly, I must first be aware of at least some of these descriptive forms.

The descriptive forms themselves appear to be a potentially infinite variety. Take one of the more simple elements in this description, namely 'bark'. Without presuming to be technically correct, one could then further describe this as being the outer covering comprising dead cells of a plant, necessarily a tree. Further define this collection of words, and one has to construe such terms as 'outer', 'covering', 'dead', 'cell' and so on. None of these terms is itself a 'simple', and to that extent incapable of further description or analysis. Further, it appears that the basis of meaning is the tautology 'A is A'. On the other hand, 'A is B' is both logically and factually false.

What about statements such as 'John is a man', or 'that ship is a schooner'? These appear to be examples of the form 'A is B'. But that shorthand is incorrect, in my opinion. Take for example 'that ship is a schooner'. Neither the word 'schooner' nor the word 'ship' itself defines the object. Each word describes a part only of the object. The word 'ship' tells us something about the object, but is insufficient in itself to define it; nor can the word 'schooner' in itself define the object. As a definition, therefore, 'the [or that] ship is a schooner' is unsatisfactory. The word 'ship', in fact, adds no further meaning in this instance than the word 'schooner', and is little short of a term which names or points to a particular object.

With regard to 'John is a man', it is the word 'man' which needs embellishment. It might be more correct or accurate to say, instead, 'John is John'. The definition would only suffice as a definition when both the definiens and the definiendum are complete and identical; in short, in the form 'A is A'. It is also unlikely that any definition is 'complete' as a definition as any such definition would be unwieldy, and therefore the definitions we create are invariably shorthand form only, and for our convenience, with a purely pragmatic objective. Take, for example, the definition of 'cat' as 'a small mammal belonging to the family *Felis catus*. Imagine how much more we would need to provide in the way of 'qualitative information' before we could be satisfied that anyone learning the word for the first time but without the aid of a 'sample', so to speak, would be surely able to identify a cat when he saw one.

If the name is used correctly, its associated definition must 'belong' only to that name, and no other – there must be no risk that the name, as defined, points to the wrong 'object'. What does this tell us about language and linguistic forms?

- That names are seldom capable of precise definition.
- That no particular or specific component of a language is by itself a picture or complete representation of any one particular or specific component of experience or perception (I was tempted to say of 'reality'). In attempting to describe an experience or a perception, each particular or specific component of a language requires us to further describe or define individual parts or the whole of that description.
- That definitions are invariably incomplete.

But it is also the case that a purported 'simple', such as a name, can be identified in a number of different ways. The question is whether any of those ways is complete in itself, or whether one is better than the other. Let's take the word 'tree' as an example. To identify our tree, we could add the word 'that', as in 'that tree'. We could say, 'tree standing at map coordinates X and Y', or 'the tree belonging to the species *Ulmus americana* (currently) standing in my back yard', or 'the tree belonging to the species *Ulmus americana* which my grandfather cut down in 1925'.

Taking a perception as an example, the structure or form of a linguistic utterance does not necessarily bear a direct relationship with that which is perceived. An example: 'I see a glass in front of me'. Here, we make a number of assumptions; the existence of space and spatial relationships; the existence of objects, namely (in this instance) the glass and its observer.

That which is perceived, if we were to describe only the perception rather than also the underlying assumptions therefrom, is shape and colour, and one could argue that shape and colour are not themselves dependent on assumptions of any kind. The observer perceives certain shapes and colours in a certain relationship with one another; though it could of course be argued that even *that* perception rests on at least one assumption, namely, the existence of a two-dimensional spatial relationship between each such colour or shape, and another colour or shape (to the right of a grey rectangular shape is a brown rectangular shape, and so on). One could argue that the observer is assuming spatial relationships between, in this case, colours and/or shapes, by describing his perceptions in such terms as this.

Subtract the observer from a statement such as this (and assume that 'objects' have an existence outwith the observer), and take as a further example the form 'the glass stands to the right of the telephone'. Or less contentiously, 'the grey rectangular shape [is] to the right of the black rectangular shape', or more simply, 'grey rectangle, right of black rectangle'.

-4-

What role, if any, does causation play in ascribing meaning to an 'utterance'?

Can all statements or propositions, without attempting to force a definition *a posteriori*, be construed to comprise, at least purportedly, statements of fact? A statement of perception will almost certainly comprise, at least purportedly, a statement of fact. But what of other categories of statement? Take, for example, a quasi-statement of perception such as 'the colours of that sunset are beautiful'. It is arguable that even the term 'beautiful' is at least in one sense a statement of fact – that which is perceived has an effect of a particular kind on the observer. Let us say the perception of the sunset causes or is, less controversially, associated with a sensation – let us say, a sensation which one can describe or indicate with the word 'happiness'. Though the term 'happiness' must itself require further analysis, assuming that that sensation is not illusory, in so far as it is unassociated with a fact (and I cannot see how it *can* be unassociated with a fact), the term 'happiness' can itself also be said to be a statement of fact.

A more abstract proposition might comprise a number of statements of fact. For example, 'God, freedom and immortality are the necessary consequences of the moral law'. So wrote Immanuel Kant. Can even any component of *this* complex statement be reduced to statements of fact? *[Note that in this extract from Kant, we appear to be concerned with metaphysically necessary consequence, rather than causally, necessary consequence.]*

Before we decide that point, I would like to suggest that in the absence of *any* relationship with a factual medium of some kind, any such statement is of doubtful significance. If that is correct, we first need to understand what we mean by 'a factual medium'.

As a first step in analysing the complex Kantian statement referred to above, one could attempt to construe the form 'necessary consequence'. Without presupposing an understanding of Kant, we could say, for example, that if X is a necessary consequence of Y, then in all cases of X, Y must have preceded. Is a temporal relationship essential to establish metaphysical necessity? What, in this context, does the word 'consequence' mean? In short, if X 'exists' or is, then Y also exists or is, at some prior time. What does that mean? Either that without Y, X would not exist, or that X is caused by, in some sense, Y – for example, as the heat from a fire causes water to boil. That the water boils is a necessary consequence of a quality contained, so to speak, in the fire. *[But here we are talking about something which is causally necessary, rather than metaphysically or logically necessary, and it seems that a causally necessary consequence is not the same as a metaphysically or logically necessary consequence.]*

In short, if Y, then X must follow, or to put this differently, if Y, then X. But the moral law, whatever that is, cannot surely precede in time, [the existence of] God. Therefore, can 'consequence', as it is used by Kant, really mean nothing more than logical consequence, or is 'metaphysical necessity' another way of saying 'definitional necessity'? It seems that we are confronted with the same fallacy which had lead to the supposition *cogito ergo sum*!

Even more problematical are the words 'God', 'freedom' and 'immortality'. If we are unable to say firstly, what these *are* or mean, and secondly, what relationship each bears with a factual medium (assuming we are satisfied with the meaning we have ascribed to the words 'factual medium'), we are surely uttering mere poetry, as it were, with perhaps the sole aim of eliciting a response in a listener. Let us suppose that we have conclusively demonstrated that 'God' has a clear connection in the realm of fact (but we cannot decide any such connection for 'freedom' or 'immortality', except that we are able to define each clearly such that a listener can understand what these words 'stand for'), we might still be able to salvage *some* meaning here. Perhaps the easiest way to give these words more than mere 'poetical' substance is to start by demonstrating that the 'realm of fact' is broad enough to contain such terms as these; that each 'exists' in some sense in the 'realm of fact'. If on the other hand, we are niggardly in fabricating our understanding of 'fact', then we may potentially shut out such *noumena* as 'God', 'freedom' and 'immortality'!

Suppose we have succeeded in understanding every component of this Kantian statement, including at minimum the words 'God', 'freedom', 'immortality', 'necessary consequence' (I suspect this has to be understood as a compound form, with a distinct meaning, *qua* compound form), and 'moral law' (another compound form). Clearly, this is an 'abstract' utterance – indeed, a highly abstract utterance – so that any conclusions as to what bearing the utterance has to 'fact' are undoubtedly not easy to draw; and yet it is also the case, surely, that in the absence of *any* bearing to the purported 'realm of fact', we ought to confine the utterance to the shelves of a disused library. In some instances, an utterance such as this may have only or primarily *one* 'bearing', namely as a spur to some form of action or behaviour; and it is that form of action or mode of behaviour which comprises the necessary connection with the realm of fact.

But come along now, are we really compelled to use such a restricted sense of the words 'realm of fact'? Can't we legitimately include abstract forms such as this as being just one more aspect of that realm? That said, if there is any reluctance to ascribe abstract statements a factual home, it is because we cannot understand the meaning of the statement in question, and/or are unable to understand what form of action or mode of behaviour it is intended to elicit, and/or (perhaps) are of the opinion that any form of action or mode of behaviour which might arise from an understanding of the statement ought not to be followed (though the last of these really does not comprise a sufficient reason to exclude the statement from the realm of fact).

-5-

Moving back to the concept of causation and the physical example of the action of fire on water, the presence of the fire and the rise in temperature of the water need not be described only or necessarily in terms of cause and effect. Rather, it is equally legitimate to define the relationship between the presence of the fire and the change in temperature of the water as merely association of the one with the other. That is to say in the circumstances where one has fire and that fire is 'applied to' or in close physical proximity to the water, one also has a change in the temperature of the water.

Even so, what causation is *not* necessarily based on is regularity or repetition; even less so, the existence of a 'law'. Therefore, the proper form should surely be 'because X, therefore Y'. But is even that wrong? The relationship should perhaps be described symbolically thus: $X \rightarrow Y$. Or 'X, then Y' (this being a temporal 'then', rather than a conditional), rather than the conditional form, 'If X then Y'.

Note that 'if X, then Y' is a predicative form, while 'because X, Y' is a descriptive form. But does the descriptive form also contain a conditional such that 'if not X, then not Y' or 'if X, then Y'?

It is not logically necessary to conclude from the circumstance of fire and its physical proximity to water that the fire has caused, in the sense that it has 'brought about', a change in the temperature of the water. That appears to be an unnecessary or illegitimate step to take. *[Comment – we are talking here of causal not logical necessity, so does that conclusion follow because causal nexus differs from logical connection?]*

Accordingly, although causation is a necessary element in the process of reasoning *[Note that this is a process concerned with logical necessity]*, 'a loss of confidence in the country's banking system gave rise to or caused a run on foreign capital', or 'the side-to-side motion of the cilia caused the organism to move in a particular direction in a fluid medium', is a non-legitimate and therefore unnecessary conclusion to draw from an observation.

However, can it be argued that that non-legitimate step plays a role in the process of reasoning such that without it one cannot appreciate the physical process it is attempting to describe? Is that step a necessary component of the statement of fact?

Consider the statement in the form 'A and B', rather than 'A therefore B' or 'If A then B'.[1] Clearly the statement 'A and B' is materially different from the statements 'A therefore B' or 'If A then B'. The association of one event or fact [?] with another event or fact [?] is quite different in kind from a circumstance in which one event or fact is caused by another event or fact.

Let us therefore examine a little more deeply the nature of causation in order that we can better appreciate that 'difference in kind'. Take the example I gave earlier of the motion of a cilium. Note that the associational form, 'sideways motion of cilium *and* unidirectional motion of organism', appears to be closer in kind to the conditional form 'if sideways motion of cilium *then* unidirectional motion of organism' than to the causative form, which is 'the sideways motion of the cilium *caused* (in the sense

---

[1] 'If A then B' has at least three distinct meanings: first, if A is the case, then B must occur also; second, that B only occurs in the event that A has also occurred; and third, that B will occur after A has occurred.

of 'brought about') the unidirectional motion of the organism'.

Both the associational form and the conditional form, when reduced to symbolical language, can be stated as follows: A + B. However, the causative form does appear to be materially different from either the associative or the conditional forms. Firstly, because it cannot be reduced to the form A + B, and secondly, because causation appears to contain within it an intuited component or an assumption; a form of 'act of creation', so to speak. We are no longer talking of two entirely separate events (or facts), albeit that the one is in some sense associated with the other; but rather, that the first in time of these events or facts, in some sense, makes or creates the second of these. *[Causation, therefore, involves greater 'integration' between the relevant events, compared to any such 'integration' between events when using the associational or conditional forms.]*

Accordingly, in symbolic terms, a causal relationship between two states of affairs could be described as: A [leads to] B, or B [derives from] A.

Apart from the conceptual form of causality, which I shall attempt to discuss further below, it appears apparent that from a common-sensical viewpoint, any two events (or states of fact) can only be perceived as in association with one another, or not in association with one another, as the case may be. If one attempted to analyse such events (or states of fact) further, one would achieve the following result.

Take as an example the following statement which appears to contain a component of causation: 'iron, when exposed to water and oxygen, forms rust – therefore, water and oxygen on the surface of an iron object *causes* the iron to rust'. In fact, we can only perceive an associative relationship in this instance, between the presence of water and oxygen on an iron surface, and the presence (some time thereafter) of rust on the same surface. So much for the perceived state of facts in this case.

Describing this state of facts with the language of causation requires us to enter the realm of hypothesis or conjecture. We hypothesise that the presence of rust on the surface of iron is the direct and necessary result of the formation of a chemical compound, comprising oxygen and iron. We cannot demonstrate this to be the case, but by way of experiment we can test our hypothesis and give it some credibility.

[But surely we can indeed 'demonstrate' this to be the case, by showing that rust is an iron oxide? Only to the extent that we can demonstrate that the oxygen in iron oxide derives from or is the same as the oxygen in water/air. We are obliged to presume that the quantities of iron and oxygen being equivalent, there is a direct relationship between the oxygen in the sample of iron oxide, and the oxygen in some other molecular form at some prior time.]

However, we are still no closer to defining cause, as all that can be gathered from this experiment (albeit a controlled experiment) is that the oxygen in air, in the presence of water 'combined' with iron to form iron oxide or rust, but that does not necessarily explain the proposition 'air and water in contact with iron, causes iron to rust'. Indeed, it is not necessary to re-state the proposition 'iron in contact with air and water forms an iron oxide' in terms of cause and effect.

[All this appears to give rise to two seperate issues: (1) How does one ascertain what caused x? And (2) what does it mean for y to cause x, or x to cause y?][2]

Can causation be proven? In short, how does one ascertain what (in fact) caused X? Take the simple statement, concealing what appears to be a causal explanation: 'smoking causes [lung] cancer'. The nature of things, and probability, being as they are, no matter how many instances we gather of the kind, 'X smoked, X contracted cancer', it remains impossible to prove thereby that smoking 'caused' or 'causes' cancer. At best, we can assert that 'in very many (or even all) perceived instances, X smoked, and X contracted cancer'.

Indeed, suppose that it can be discovered, incontrovertibly, that the presence of chemical φ is found in every case of a particular form of cancer, and that chemical φ is also found in cigarette smoke. Does that bring us any closer to the required proof? Unfortunately not, because even that discovery is an instance of the form of proposition above, 'chemical φ in the cancer, and chemical φ in the cigarette smoke'. One would need to make a further non-necessary or illegitimate assumption in order to conclude that 'chemical φ causes cancer'.

[note also Wittgenstein's point that causation is incapable

---

2 But note that even though we may not understand what it means for X to cause Y, there may be some utility in maintaining that Y and X are 'related in some causal sense' (albeit that we do not understand that) if we can be sure that the one event occurs in the presence of the other.

of proof as it involves a prediction of a future event]

So what then do we, or would we, mean by the statement 'chemical φ causes cancer'? Is it that in the absence of chemical φ, there would not be a cancer, or at least a particular form of cancer? Are we saying 'no chemical φ, no cancer ρ'? Not necessarily, if what we are attempting to do is define causation, because we might discover instances where chemical φ was present, but no cancer ρ, or where cancer ρ was found, but no chemical φ.

Could we describe the above process in reverse order, so to speak? 'No cancer ρ, no chemical φ'. This does not make intuitive sense, and the reason for this is the necessarily asymmetrical relationship which we would be attempting to describe above, bound up also with our concept of time, as intuitively perceived, process and sequence.

Is it possible then, to go any further than the statement that 'chemical φ is found to be [in certain, many, or even all discovered cases] associated with cancer ρ'? In short, 'chemical φ, [and] cancer ρ'. The process of inductive reasoning being what it is, we could always envisage a situation where cancer ρ existed even in the absence of chemical φ.

But suppose we discover even just the one instance of cancer ρ where no chemical φ were to be found. That would not demonstrate, therefore, that chemical φ did not cause cancer ρ. Indeed, the existence of that one instance of cancer ρ in the absence of chemical φ merely suggests, or could be a means of showing, that cancer ρ may have more than one cause, albeit that one such cause is indeed chemical φ.

We return therefore, to our attempt to encapsulate the concept of causation.

[but consider that while logical necessity may be conceivable, causal necessity appears to be a chimera]

What is meant by the statement that two or more events are associated with one another? Surely the concept of association is as much a chimera as is the concept of cause? What we intend to say, surely, is that in all perceived instances of X, Y was also perceived. That observation neither proves nor disproves causation. 'If X exists, then Y exists' is very close in form to 'X causes Y to exist'.

-6-

Though it may not seem possible to prove the existence of causation, it does appear to be possible, at least conceptually, to show that in any one instance or compound event, one component of that event or instance could cause (in the sense of 'bring about') another. Conceptually, when we speak of X event causing Y event, what we appear to mean is that in that particular instance, X event was a necessary precursor to Y event. (Surely, there is one additional assumption involved in causation, and that is that the effect was brought about by its cause, as even two associated events can be envisaged by way of 'necessary precursor' language). Analysing this further, in that instance, Y event would not have occurred had X event not occurred prior to that. Or to be more exact, Y event would not have occurred, *in this instance*, had X event not occurred prior to that. That is to say that in different circumstances it is conceivable that Y event may have occurred because of some *other* prior event. But in *this* instance, had X event not occurred, Y event would not have followed. [Is this what is meant by a sufficient condition?]

Take another example: a lightning strike upon the earth, following which the tinder catches fire. Many things will contribute to the tinder catching fire, but it would appear that were it not for the lightning (though the tinder was indeed dry and combustible, and therefore capable of conflagration), the tinder would not have lit at all. Is the necessary cause of an event no more than that event which is closest in time to the conflagration? It is arguable that only the last in a series of events appears to be the proximate cause of the conflagration. So it cannot be said that the cause of the conflagration was the dryness of the tinder, but merely that it was a sufficient condition of the conflagration. To that extent, it is true that the conflagration would not have occurred were it not that the tinder was sufficiently dry, but however dry that tinder was, it would not have caught fire, were it not for the lightning that struck it, no differently than if a flame from a candle (or some other source of heat) had been applied to the tinder.

Likewise, if we consider again my earlier example, that of the association of chemical φ and cancer ρ, it is feasible that chemical φ is the proximate cause of that cancer, in so far as cancer ρ would not have developed at all were it not for the presence of chemical φ in the relevant individual's body. It is, of course, conceivable that cancer ρ could develop in the absence of chemical φ, but it is conceivable that cancer ρ has more than one possible proximate cause, just as the conflagration of the dry tinder may have more than one proximate cause, but without any such proximate cause, cancer ρ and the conflagration would not occur.

Three points, however, on proof (and this lies at the core of inductive enquiry): first, that no matter how many cases we witness of the association of cancer ρ and chemical φ, we are unable to state with certainty or to prove that cancer ρ was caused by chemical φ; second, we are unable, at least through observation only, to prove even that chemical φ is *a* cause of cancer ρ, in so far as chemical φ brings about or makes, so to speak, cancer ρ; and third, that no matter how many instances we note of the presence of chemical φ in cancer ρ, we are unable to predict or state that all instances of cancer ρ will contain, and even less so, were caused, by chemical φ.[3]

To that extent it is also illegitimate to speak of the laws of nature, or indeed of the laws of physics, because what comprises a law in that case is merely an assumption borne of a multitude of observations, and a further assumption that every such observation was similar to or even the same as each other.

Clearly, two events being merely associated with one another cannot be said to be the same as one event bringing about, or 'making', another event.

What then is the difference between events being associated with one another, and events being in a causal relationship with one another? Is it even legitimate to say

---

[3] We are also unable to infer, therefore, that chemical φ was a *cause of* cancer ρ.

that two events can merely be 'associated' with one another, in the sense that if one event occurs, the other event is also likely, or even certain, to occur? Let us take a hypothetical circumstance where if one event occurs, another particular event always occurs also. Isn't this what we mean when we speak of one event as causing another? If the two events are always associated one with another, in the sense that if one occurs, the other also occurs (and we are assuming that these two occurrences will necessarily be proximate to one another, both spatially as well as temporally) then that is what we mean, surely, when we speak in terms of one event causing, or bringing about, another event. We cannot *see* the one event literally causing or bringing about the other, but given our state of knowledge of these events, and a certain degree of hypothesising, we assume that the one event causes the other.

We note innumerable instances where water meeting with the surface of iron, in the presence of air, after the passage of time results in a coating of what we call 'rust' on that surface. We cannot literally see the interaction of the iron with the air and water, and the assumption of cause is in this instance based on the theory of molecular interaction. We offer an explanation for the occurrence of the substance we call 'rust' on the surface of iron by positing that an 'interaction' occurs between components of iron, and necessarily also components of water and air, to result in the substance we call 'rust'. To that extent, we say that the rust was caused by the interaction of a number of chemicals or substances. Alternatively, we might say that the interaction of these chemicals or substances *resulted in* the rust – a more passive form of the same description.[4]

But, if instead of stating that one event caused another event we state that one event resulted in another, we are surely saying no more than that one event was (seen to be) associated with another event.

However, if we take an example not from the field of chemistry, where it may be difficult or philosophically impossible to demonstrate that one event has caused another, but from, say, the realm of human endeavour, it may be possible to try to characterise cause and effect with more precision.

Take as an example 'James turned the key, and thereby locked the door'. The events which this describes can be re-stated, as follows. 'The turning of the key clockwise (by James) caused the cam within the door-lock to turn in a clockwise direction, and the cylindrical latch to move to the right and into the slot in the door frame, rendering the door immobile'. Here, we do appear to have a clear sequence and set of events where each event appears to be preceded, and is caused by, another event.

I suggest that the reason why *this* set of events can be more easily construed as an instance of causation is on the basis that it requires human intervention and concerns an intentional act.

On the other hand, if we were to consider any set or apparent set of events where no form of human intervention

---

[4] Rust is caused by virtue of a chemical reaction between iron, oxygen and water. The chemical composition of rust is hydrated iron oxide. Iron oxide is composed of atoms of iron and oxygen. Therefore, iron + oxygen + water = rust. In symbolic form: Rust = $Fe + O_2 + H_2O$ (or $Fe_2O_3.nH_2O$)

was evident, it is *a priori* impossible to demonstrate with certainty that any one event in that set is caused by any other preceding event. It is only possible to claim that one event is always or generally preceded or followed by another event. We are unable to demonstrate that an event is the cause of the event which follows and is associated with it.

If we are unable to demonstrate or to prove that an event is the cause of another event which follows it, it is surely unnecessary for us to speak in terms of an event causing another event. It is sufficient, on the other hand, to speak in terms of associated events, purely on the grounds that the two events generally or always occur in association with one another, which leads us to conclude that there is a probability (or perhaps only a possibility) that when the first in time occurs, this will be followed by the second event.

Can it, however, be shown that it is *a priori* impossible to define cause and effect, except perhaps in the context of the actions of animate (though not necessarily conscious) beings? If it can be shown that cause and effect has meaning only in relation to an action, rather than an event in the absence of an action, we are some way towards showing that cause and effect can only be defined in terms of the special 'sub-category' of event known as actions. If we begin by defining an action as an event of an animate being and an event as a state of affairs involving an occurrence in space and time (which we can distinguish from a state of affairs per se, or in short, a fact): 'brown carpet' is a fact, rather than an event; 'rainfall' is an event, as well as a fact.

Two questions: first, is motion or change the essential feature of an event? Second, does each event contain at least one fact? Or is it the case that facts and events are mutually exclusive?

Take rainfall as an instance of event. It is possible to construe 'aspects' of this event as fact. For example, the colour, texture or temperature of the substance we call rain. Note that it is not the concept of rainfall which can be construed as fact; rather, it is the event of rainfall which 'contains' or comprises a number of facts – colour, temperature, and so on.

Causation does not concern facts per se; but a fact can be caused by another fact, or more correctly, by an event. Accordingly, the temperature of the rain is (one can argue) caused by (the exact means of which will necessitate describing this event in terms of a physical process) ultraviolet radiation from the sun.

Though temperature may itself be construed as a fact, it can also be described as an event if one attempts to analyze temperature as the direct result of a physical process, or in short, an event (for example, a postulated sub-atomic event or process).

Taken at the level of physical processes invisible to the naked eye, a fact is capable of further analysis and can be described as an event or the consequence of an event, or a number of events. However, that event or collection of events is itself incapable of proof or verification.

Although we are unable to prove that one event is the cause of another event, and accordingly demonstrate the existence of causation, the assumption or hypothesis of causation is a necessary step in predicting events, and a necessary element in the process of reasoning.

Accordingly, the concept of causation is a mere convenience by virtue of which we carry out the mental processes of analysis and prediction. We assume that because in a large number of instances of cancer ρ, we also detect or perceive chemical φ, chemical φ causes in some sense the outcome, namely cancer ρ, such that if we were to detect or perceive chemical φ, or better still, the source of chemical φ in any one organism, we could predict or assume further that that organism could contract cancer ρ (assuming also, for the sake of argument, that chemical φ was further assumed to be the, or a proximate or necessary, cause of cancer ρ, rather than merely associated with cancer ρ, such that in the absence of chemical φ, cancer ρ would not result).

But perhaps we have too easily admitted defeat, and causation really *is* capable of definition or meaning. Take as an example a common observation – the wind causes the dust to shift from one place to the next. We know, at least intuitively, that we perceive not merely an association between the wind or the action of the wind, and the movement of the dust. We appear to perceive that it is the wind itself which, so to speak, lifts the dust from one location to another, and this is demonstrated in a number of ways – first, if the wind dies down, the dust ceases to move, or moves only when the wind reaches a particular velocity; second, the direction or trajectory of the wind is approximately identical to the direction or trajectory of the dust.

However, notwithstanding the highly persuasive nature of these observations, I suggest that even in an instance of this kind, we are required to take an illegitimate step from the observation of two separate processes – atmospheric movement and the motion of particles of dust, to the conclusion that the one process occurred because the other process preceded or accompanied it, such that the first of these would not have occurred, but for the occurrence of the second, and further than that, that the second made the first occur. What is difficult to demonstrate conclusively or otherwise, is precisely that; namely, that one event made the other event occur. Through observation alone, all we can conclusively state is that the one event preceded the other or was contiguous in time, and further than that, that in a number of, or even all, perceived instances, the two events were, in that manner, associated with one another. Each event occurred in relation to the other.

Beyond that statement of observation, we enter the realms of hypothesis or conjecture, when we attempt to describe the way in which the one event makes or leads the other; for example, the action of wind on dust, where we posit, for example, qualities of a gas or mixture of gases such as the atmosphere is composed of in relation to solid objects.[5]

If we cannot understand what causation means, we are obliged to admit that a necessary basis of the process of reasoning is *sans* a clear foundation.

---

[5] Further analysis: – see Appendix

Facts and Events

I have made frequent reference to 'fact' in the foregoing sections of this book. The time has come to try to understand the word better!

My principal aim in this section is to juxtapose 'fact' with 'event'. It may appear, therefore, that what I mean by 'fact' is some form of physical or perceivable 'state of affairs'. But I think the word 'fact' is capable of a much broader definition than that.

Instead, I define 'fact' as any passive description of the world we occupy. Therefore, a thought or thought process, abstract or otherwise, is a 'fact'. But if a thought or thought process is capable of being defined as a 'fact', then only the passive description of that thought will comprise fact.

-2-

How does a statement of fact differ from an event, and is it even necessary to distinguish one from the other?

A statement of fact may be defined as a non-temporal

statement, for example, 'black cat'; whilst an event may be defined as containing a temporal aspect, perhaps necessarily a spatio-temporal aspect, for example, 'black cat walking'.

That said, the defining feature of a statement of fact would appear to be direct correspondence with the perception of *something*. A statement of fact is not defined by way of its linguistic form; accordingly, the statement 'slithey toad' would not be a statement of fact, because the word 'slithey' has neither meaning nor any correspondence with a perceived circumstance, notwithstanding that the word 'toad' corresponds to the perception of a certain kind of animal. The misuse of language, notwithstanding apparent correctness of form, is also capable of meaninglessness. Accordingly, 'cavernous toad' is correct in form but *sans* meaning, except as some kind of poetical utterance!

The simplest form of a statement of fact would appear to comprise a naming word, such as cat, and in so far as that word is used in such a manner as to make it clear that it concerns a particular perceived object; for example, as an exclamatory utterance such as 'cat!' upon seeing the animal in one's midst, that word suffices as a statement of fact.

More typically, however, the statement of fact will provide some detail or embellishment to the mere naming word in order to comprise a statement of fact.

Statements of fact can be further divided into statements of particular fact, for example, 'that black cat', and statements of general fact, such as 'cats like milk'.

An event is a statement of fact containing a (spatio-)temporal aspect; for example, 'Alexander crossed the Hellespont in 334 B.C.E.', or 'black cat drinking milk'.

Both these statements of event contain a verb, but (bearing in mind that a statement of event contains a temporal aspect) is a verb, or the equivalent, a necessary component of a statement of event?

It is possible to construct an event using a set or series of statements of fact, each without a verb, as follows: 'black cat's head close to bowl'; 'black cat's tongue protruding'; 'black cat's tongue in milk'; 'black cat's tongue protracted'.

The event sentence, 'black cat drinking milk', in fact contains that set or series of statements of fact, and only has meaning in as far as we understand the meaning of each such statement of fact.

Notwithstanding our ability to describe the spatial aspect of an event as a set or series of statements of fact, that set or series of statements of fact also needs to contain a temporal aspect in order to represent a true statement of event.

Arguably, the set or series of statements of fact which we have set out here, if connected to one another by temporal words such as 'then', 'after that', 'followed by' and so on, should go some way towards the formation of a statement of event.

Is an event or a statement of event, necessarily also a *historical* event, which is to say a factual circumstance which takes place in space and time, albeit in an imaginary or conceived space and time?

If we define an event or statement of event as a fact or series or set of facts which contains a spatio-temporal dimension, then by virtue of its having a spatio-temporal dimension, an event or statement of event is necessarily a historical event (a historical event being, by definition, an event which takes place in space and time) and presupposes a spatio-temporal medium in which events occur, at least on a conceptual level.

I have defined an event as necessarily being a set or series of facts comprising a process. As a consequence, an event is inconceivable as a singular or 'momentary' state of affairs – that would, on the contrary, be a *fact*, as I have defined this.

Causation, in its conceptual form, is dependent on the existence of process, such as we conceive underlies our understanding of *event*, as I have defined this. But process, as I have defined this, is a fiction necessitated by the manner in which the mind functions. Accordingly, the statement of fact 'black cat' does not contain, nor can it contain, a statement of causation. Nor would a statement of fact describing more than one object (for example, 'black cat on rug') contain a statement of causation as one cannot, at least on a common-sensical level, argue that the cat and the rug are in a causal relationship with one another, as so described.

Further embellishment of that statement may bring us closer to describing just such a relationship; so, for example, 'the black cat on the rug [and] changes to the outer form of the rug underneath the black cat', or in short, the weight and shape of the cat has caused the rug to change its shape or contour.

Though baldly stated, the statement 'black cat on rug has changed the outer form of rug underneath black cat' does not appear to be itself a statement of event, in so far as the black cat lying on the rug has 'caused' a change to the form of that rug, which in the absence of the black cat, or any substitute therefor, would not have occurred.

However, upon further analysis, it is clear that that statement is closely related to the statement of event, 'the black cat [or more precisely, the form and weight of the cat] caused the outer form of the rug to change'. Undoubtedly, the nature of that change can be described more fully; it is sufficient for my purposes to use instead the shorthand form 'change'.

[Consider also the concept of 'reverse causation', which is counter-intuitive on two grounds – firstly, because of the assumption I have described above with respect to forward causation, but secondly, because it is temporally difficult to sustain.]

On Sense and Nonsense

Distinguishing between sense and nonsense could be conceived of as a step towards identifying a truth.

But before we relegate nonsense to the waste disposal cart, it may help to ask if even nonsense is entirely without meaning, or, let us say, purpose? Is the purpose of a statement or communication the key quality it must have in order for it to have 'significance'? The word 'significance' is with various meanings and it is perhaps almost impossible to agree a principle sense of the word.

If we are concerned with factual or historical events, and I do not deny that (like 'significance') the sense of the word 'fact' is itself difficult to agree, then our statements must be a genuine reflection of those events. If our statements are either an embellishment, or a fabrication or falsification of events, then I would argue that our statements are without significance.

Much more could be said about historical statements – what they comprise, and their purpose and significance, but that is not the purpose of this section.

What is it we value in a historical statement, which we assume is missing in a fabrication or fantasy?

For the sake of argument, let me define historical fact as a fact which is one of three kinds:

- a fact which concerns something which I assume is "physically 'external'" to me as an observer; or
- a fact which concerns something which I assume is "physically" performed by me, as an actor and an observer; or
- a fact which comprises a thought process or sensation.

It may be possible to gather evidence of either of the first two of these – we might construe the activity of gathering evidence as a process of verification or confirmation of the fact.

On the other hand, facts which concern solely the 'inner world' of thought or sensation cannot be subjected to checks for any correspondence between the thought or sensation and anything else; and to that extent, it is not possible to decide whether any statement of any such inner world thought or sensation is sense or nonsense (but is such correspondence, or even coherence, key?).

As a consequence, there is little we can do or say to confirm the sense (that is to say either the meaning or the veracity) of an inner world statement. Indeed, it may not even make sense to try to confirm the sense of an inner world statement. They are what they are. We could perhaps simply consider them as telling us something about the terrain or topography of the inner world.

Of course, it is tempting to argue instead that there is in fact no material difference between an inner and an outer world statement – save that the outer world statement appears to assume the existence of something other than an inner world 'sensation'.

Notwithstanding, perhaps we should focus our attention on statements which purport to say something about the so-called 'outer world': the world of things or objects external to our consciousness. Of course, the outer world is created from a number of individual perceptions and assumptions (they are of course nothing short of 'inner world' activities); but assuming its existence, our statements concerning the outer world must surely correspond to (or at least reflect) something about the outer world. But what of the category of statements called 'judgements' or 'opinion'? It is difficult, or even perhaps a waste of effort, to seek correspondence between a judgement or opinion and the outer world - or is it? If our judgement or opinion is widely considered to be unsubstantiated, or worse still, incorrect, then surely what that means in other words is that there is no, or insufficient, 'correspondence' between our judgement or opinion and the outer world which it concerns, or purports to reflect. In other words, what would it mean for a judgement or opinion to be described as unfounded or incorrect or implausible? Take as an example an opinion (little more, really, than a 'belief') that all members of X race of *Homo sapiens* exhibit certain qualities. If it can be shown that in fact they do not, or more probably that there are only some who do, but most or many do not, then our opinion is incorrect, or only partially correct and requires modification.

But when we compare one thing with another, we

appear to be unable to assert the truth or falsehood of either thing. The act of comparison has the same fundamental flaws as the act of correspondence in the correspondence theory of truth. At its basis, this is an act of drawing a comparison between a statement, and something else.

Correspondence and Verification

What does 'correspondence' comprise in the context of epistemology? Broadly, that X, as a statement or description, 'corresponds' with Y, a presumed state of affairs. The difficulty of course is in understanding what it means for a statement to 'correspond' to a state of affairs! We can, however, go some way towards demonstrating whether the presumption of a certain state of affairs is justified or correct.

As for 'verification', broadly speaking, in this context this will comprise the 'confirmation' or 'truth' of a statement, for example by virtue of either (a) correspondence with a presumed state of affairs, or (b) some other form of 'correspondence'. How do they differ, and to what extent is it feasible to perform the test in question? In any event, there is no reason why we cannot use different 'tests' in different circumstances.

What does correspondence entail, and how does it differ from verification? What should correspond with what, in order for this process to be complete: the statement or proposition with the fact or event? If yes, how is that correspondence demonstrated?

Examples:

(a) 'it is raining' by, for example, stepping outdoors and seeing if we get wet;
(b) 'Socrates is a man' by, for example, showing that Socrates was married to Callista, a woman, and that they had children by one another.

Isn't this verification, rather than correspondence? The base requirement seems to be: demonstrate the truth of the statement or proposition. That there is a need to demonstrate the truth of a statement or proposition should be clear; in the absence of this, we would all be at the mercy of the fabricators, and at minimum, unable to distinguish between truth and falsehood.

So, the question is whether the principle of verification, introduced by the logical positivists, is incorrect and must be abandoned, or whether it contains some value but needs modification, or whether there is some better way to demonstrate the truth or falsehood of an assertion.

Does the process of verification or confirmation, call it what one will, and whatever form this may take, rely in some sense on the notion of an objective world or objects; or is it the case that whatever the underlying belief is, the process of verification or confirmation remains the same?

This is unlikely, because it is precisely because we believe in a world of objects outwith the 'subject' that we have devised a method by which we look for 'correspondence' between an assertion, statement or proposition, and that world of objects.

Correspondence and Verification

What are the common meanings of the words 'to verify'? To check; to confirm; to test. The key question, surely, is how that is done, and whether there are valid and possibly also invalid methods by which to verify something.

A related question is 'what exactly is it that is being verified, or in need of verification?' If the answer to that is 'the truth of the statement in question', we are confronted again with the first question, namely 'how is verification done?'

A statement such as 'the tree is ten feet tall' is verified quite simply by measurement – albeit that one could object that the statement is incorrect in so far as it cannot be shown that the tree is *exactly* ten feet tall; that it is likely to be somewhat less or somewhat more than this; therefore that the statement is false. But undoubtedly that is a rather facile comment to make. Our descriptions of the world and our use of language are almost always approximate only, and to that extent, if the tree is arguably 10.002 feet tall, it is for all purposes correct to describe it as being ten feet tall.

Of course, there are a number of types of statement which are in principle incapable of verification of any kind, simply because we do not know *how* to make the required checks and tests, or we cannot be agreed as to which tests are applicable, or the tests we have fashioned are of only partial help in testing the truth of the statement we are concerned with.

So, for example, historical statements such as 'the German dictator Adolf Hitler travelled from Spain to Argentina in 1945'. The statement is not without meaning;

in fact, the meaning of the statement should be patently clear. What is problematical is the confirmation or denial of the truth of the statement. Evidence can support the case for its truth, but no quantity or type of evidence can or is capable of providing confirmation, as such. The most we can say is that the evidence strongly supports, or somesuch, the truth of the statement.

A particular category of historical or quasi-historical statement is even more problematical, and that is the type of statement which purports to describe an event or a fact which took place prior to any recorded testimony, or in short a 'pre-historical' event. For example, that 'the dinosaurs became extinct as a direct result of the impact on the surface of the earth of a large extra-terrestrial object'.

An increasingly problematical type of historical statement, indeed a type of quasi-historical statement, is a statement of theoretical physics or theoretical cosmology, such as 'space, time and matter had its beginning in the big bang'.

The conclusion we can draw from this attempted analysis of historical and quasi-historical statements is that like all 'beliefs', they are *a priori* incapable of confirmation. Rather, like evidence adduced in a criminal matter, no quantity of any such evidence can *conclusively* demonstrate the truth of an allegation.

There is no one method by which to distinguish sense from nonsense. Indeed it is foolish to seek a unitary, one-size-fits-all type of system.

It is necessary to distinguish between fantasy and the process of reasoning. It is assumed that the first of these

Correspondence and Verification

has no basis or no explicit basis in fact, and the second is a (genuine) attempt to explain or to draw conclusions *from* the facts.

I can conceive of the moon as being formed of cheddar cheese, or of a beast with the upper body of a man and the lower body of a goat; that these comprise 'fantasies' is easily demonstrated in either case, and generally this is done by showing that the moon is composed at least largely of rock, and that no such beast exists or has been found to exist, nor is it consistent with our experience that any such beast could exist. In short, we demonstrate the fantastical nature of our thoughts by pointing specifically to some fact or facts, or the absence of something in the factual realm.

A process of reasoning, however, will concern facts as its basis, and to the extent that it strays from the factual, it loses cogency.

For example, 'there was a confluence of cold with warm air over the Pacific Ocean'; this is the first observation or fact. 'Heavy rain fell over the X landmass'; this is fact number two. We are led to conclude that the confluence of cold and warm air over the ocean caused or brought about the precipitation of rainfall over X landmass, this being an instance of the process of reasoning.

On the other hand, if I had said instead that the god of rain was angry (or for that matter, pleased) with the people of X landmass, and as a consequence had 'caused' rain to fall on them, I have said something which can be neither confirmed nor denied, nor demonstrated. But this, too, follows the same process of reasoning, surely?

But why do I suppose that the process of reasoning

has anything to do with facts? If the process of reasoning contains non-factual or fantastical information, any conclusions drawn thereby will surely be false: 'all men have three kidneys; John is a man; therefore, John has three kidneys'. Can I say, citing the cosmological argument for the existence of God, that that process of reasoning, being based on factual information, is materially different from fantasy? Isn't it possible to draw a conclusion which strays from the factual, notwithstanding that the key premises in that argument are themselves statements of fact? My chapter *An Essay on Epistemology* explores this point also.

Perhaps we should focus on trying to better understand what constitutes knowledge, and what comprises truth. These are questions which are different from the question 'how do we distinguish between a meaningful and a meaningless utterance?' Yes, utterance, not proposition. Sense and nonsense are therefore the two key concepts to define.

Utility or usefulness sometimes plays a part in whether we consider something (generally something set in language with a cultural basis) 'meaningful'. So, for example, an anthropologist may argue that certain myths have a distinct purpose or utility in or for a particular society (see Levi Strauss) which we may also describe as their function.

Likewise, as parents, we may create fantastical stories when we wish to convey a particular mode of thought or behaviour to our children. We may, for example, tell our children that if they misbehave in a particular way, the consequence thereof will be something quite fearful to the mind of a child.

Correspondence and Verification

In cases like this (whether a myth vociferously adhered to by an entire society or a mere fiction told to a child), though the description in question bears little or no correspondence to 'fact' and the truth of the description is largely incapable of demonstration, the reason why we do not condemn such matters to the realm of nonsense is because of the utility of the matter, not its veracity. But why should utility matter?

The question one should ask is not whether these matters should be discarded on the grounds of meaninglessness, but rather whether they should be discarded on the grounds of the absence of any purpose or utility. If it can be shown that the purpose itself is flawed, or a 'better' conflicting purpose should replace it, then we have grounds to discard the matter in question. Similarly, and on similar grounds, we select and discard an explanation.

Obviously, not all utterances (or statements or propositions) concern matters of fact, or matters which can be perceived, demonstrated or 'verified'. But for those categories of utterance which are non-factual (the societal myth; the salutary tale told to a child) the question should always be 'what is the purpose or function of the utterance, and is that purpose or function itself defensible?'

What I object to, however, is the passing-off of a non-truth as though it were a fact. If something comprises a fact, then it should be capable of being subjected to the kinds of test which facts are subjected to in order to ascertain their veracity. For a statement (or a description) to purport to be a fact and yet to be in principle incapable of any form of credible testing, is indefensible. And what comprises a 'defensible' purpose or function? Perhaps when deciding that question, we inadvertently enter the area of ethics and leave epistemology behind!

The veracity of historical statements is notoriously difficult to test, but we do indeed subject historical statements to various forms of test; we seek documentary and physical (including geological or archaeological) evidence to test the veracity of a historical statement, and if evidence in support is insufficient or unavailable then we conclude (indeed, we ought to conclude) that that statement is unsupported, and therefore of doubtful veracity.

Any historical statement must, at basis, also contain nothing which is physically or notionally impossible. (See my commentary on the subject of miracle or 'revelation'.) Therefore, an assertion which states that the Kennedy brothers in the United States of America were the subject of 'mysterious' forces, and that is why they met untimely or 'unnatural' deaths, is not a historical statement at all, although it purports to be a historical statement, because it contains a pseudo-observation (the presence of 'mysterious' forces) which by definition are or appear to be incapable of confirmation, description or comprehension. In so far as the existence or presence of 'mysterious' forces is incapable of confirmation, description or comprehension, this pseudo-historical statement fails to adhere to one of the most fundamental presuppositions of any historical statement; namely, that what gives rise to the fact or facts it describes must not run counter to that which we typically observe to be the case, must not to that extent be absurd, and must

Correspondence and Verification

be capable of some kind or level of confirmation. But why should this be the case? There is surely no reason why a non-typical observation should be construed as *a priori* absurd, or why an explanation such as this must confirm prior observation. Surely the reason why we reject this kind of explanation is because it cannot be tested or confirmed? We cannot observe or test for 'mysterious forces'. We do not even know what any such forces comprise or mean.

It might help also to understand what we mean by 'absurd'. What is an absurd description or an absurd statement of purported fact? Nothing more, surely, than a description or statement which is in some sense contrary to observation, or contrary to common observation. An example of this is as follows: 'it is raining cats and dogs'.

We understand 'cats' and 'dogs' to refer to two distinct species of small land-based mammal, and 'rain' to refer to water falling to earth from a particular kind of cloud formation, in particular atmospheric conditions.

'Cats' and 'dogs', therefore, cannot, by definition, comprise 'rain', and even if we *were* to construe the word 'raining' in this case as though it was a metaphor for precipitation earthwards from (as it were) the 'heavens', we simply do not (ordinarily) observe cats and dogs falling earthwards from the heavens, and it would therefore be advisable to deem any such statement of purported observation as being absurd.

At one remove from a historical statement is a statement containing an ethical principle. For example, that 'it is wrong to injure or kill another individual'. It is not possible to re-word this moral principle as though it were a statement of fact. The difficulty here lies in understanding words such as 'wrong' (or its corollary 'right') or words with a common import or meaning with 'wrong' or 'right' – for example, 'ought not' or 'should'. Words such as these are guides to action, rather than a description of a particular state of affairs. Indeed, they are words whose aim is to *bring about* a particular state of affairs, in so far as the imperative they each contain is followed.

Underlying statements such as this is a belief or an opinion, for example, that the death of an individual is objectionable or undesirable, in contrast to his subsistence; or that life (human life, for example) is inviolable, or some such.

It is precisely because statements such as this are non-factual, or alternatively because they contain a component of belief or opinion, that it is *a priori* impossible to view them as necessarily or universally applicable. It is always conceivable (perverse though that conception may be) that the death of an individual at the hands of another is utterly benign. Or, to take a moral statement which is indeed difficult to settle: the killing of an unborn foetus is wrong. The reason why it is so difficult to settle a statement such as this is because it is, for one thing, impossible to decide what constitutes a person or an individual, such that their life is in some sense inviolable and therefore must be protected; impossible, because it is largely a matter of opinion, not a matter of fact, as to what constitutes a person or an individual.

And opinion and belief are indeed bedfellows, because belief also is notoriously difficult to either refute (refute is probably not even the appropriate word) or confirm. Beliefs and opinions simply do not lend themselves to refutation or confirmation – they quite simply 'subsist', whether or not attempts are made, vain or otherwise, to refute or confirm them. That is because refutation and confirmation are activities which have application only to that sub-set of affirmations we call statements of fact. As a consequence, there is a danger that any opinion or belief can be espoused, as there really is nothing we can say or do to conclusively do away with that opinion or belief.

Knowledge and Belief

The term 'belief' has at least the following two senses:

- Believing that something is *appropriate* in the circumstances; for example, a belief that vitamin C is 'good' for me if I am nursing a cold.
- Believing that something is the case; for example, believing that I am currently seated in a chair.

The second of these two senses is what most of us would ordinarily describe as 'knowledge'; but it is probably closer in kind to an assumption only, and should in principle be distinguished from knowledge. The first of these is, at best, based on some form of 'knowledge' in the second sense.

'Knowledge', as the word is typically used, appears to imply a kind of certainty or something indubitable. When I say that I am currently seated in a chair, the implication is that I am certain that this is the case, indeed that it would be absurd for anyone to dispute this. For most people, to doubt this would be to raise a very odd objection to what is quite conclusive – an objection better reserved for idle philosophical introspection! But on reflection, though I (or my observer) seem convinced that I am currently seated in a chair, this is not a matter of which either of us can be certain. Any such perception or observation is capable of error, and to that extent a 'belief' in the second sense of the word can hardly have the same implication as 'knowledge'.

And that begs the question as to what 'knowledge' is, and how it differs from 'belief'. As these words are commonly used, it seems that knowledge describes a mental state in which it is supposed that the contents of that knowledge, or perhaps the state itself, are free of error, or the risk of error, so to speak.

On reflection, surely the only state of mind (call it 'knowledge') which is supposedly *a priori* incapable of error is knowledge by definition, or in Kantian terms, *a priori* analytic assertions; for example, that my father's brother is my uncle; or that the numbers two and two, added together, equal the number four. All else appears to be belief, and is by definition capable of error or disproof.

I do not and cannot *know* that the man standing before me is my uncle – I believe that he is, though there are circumstances in which I would sound downright perverse to deny this; but in so far as my belief can be mistaken, notwithstanding that I say that I am quite sure that he is, I would be foolish to give the assertion the status of knowledge.

A person might argue that all I have done is re-defined the word 'knowledge' to exclude many of the types of assertion which we typically otherwise include in our definition of the word. On the contrary, I am concerned with ensuring that we fully understand what we mean when we say we 'know' something to be the case. I refer to the definitions of 'to know' as 'to be certain', or 'to have information in your mind', rather than 'to know how [to] …', or 'to be familiar with' something. If we are strict with our use of the word 'know' in these two senses, then we are unable to apply it to anything except knowledge by definition.

A belief, therefore, being capable of error or disproof, can (I suggest) never constitute knowledge – alternatively, we should define knowledge in a rather messy manner to include a range or a mix of meaning, some as-is, and others only perhaps. That is unhelpful, and I suggest therefore that that definition of knowledge should not be followed.

Theories of Truth

(A) Correspondence

We are unable to perceive anything but our perceptions. That is an obvious tautology, but I suggest that it is a tautology which warrants expression.

If we assume an external and objective universe, we are unable to say anything about it except that which our perceptions can tell us. Therefore we are unable to form any kind of correspondence between our perceptions and the purported 'external' world.

The correspondence theory of truth contains a major flaw, namely that it cannot enable us to ascertain what the 'actual state of affairs' is. We are therefore unable to form a 'correspondence' between a statement or proposition and that which the statement or proposition concerns because the theory presupposes a knowledge of 'objective reality'.

That said, our inability to say anything about the 'real world' does not prevent us from drawing some form of correspondence or confluence with our perceptions.

Any theory of truth, if it is to be workable, must

contain a clear notion of what it is that actually 'carries' a truth – let us call this 'a truth carrier'; so, for example, a statement or assertion in a natural language can be a truth carrier. As a subsequent step, any theory of truth must also enable the user to confirm the 'truth' contained in any one truth carrier.

In order to do this, the user will need to understand what he means by 'truth', and also how that act of 'confirmation' is carried out. Because a truth carrier can be of a variety of types, it is unlikely that the word 'truth' will have the same meaning in each case; and it is also unlikely that the act of confirmation will be the same in each case.

A truth carrier such as 'it is now raining in London', contains a number of 'truth components', namely: an observation of a phenomenon we call 'rain'; an understanding of the meaning of the word 'now'; and an appreciation of 'London' as a word signifying a determinable location on planet Earth possessing a determinable and finite boundary. The act of 'first-hand' confirmation in this case should not be difficult, and will consist of the making of an observation.

A truth carrier such as '$(x + 2)(x - 2) = x^2 - 4$' contains truth components which are confirmed or proved in a manner very different from the example I have given above.

The flaws in the correspondence theory of truth, namely that its underlying assumptions of an objective reality, or an 'actual state of affairs', are themselves apparently incapable of confirmation and remain mere assumptions, warrant examination. That said, the principle on which the correspondence theory is based – that there must be some

Theories of Truth

'correspondence', or as I have called this, 'confirmation', between the relevant truth carrier and something else – has value. One difficulty arises because that 'something else' will, as I have said, differ from one truth carrier to another; it may not therefore be possible to discover a general principle applicable to all truth carriers.

I think all we can say with confidence is that any 'correspondence' or 'coherence' is essentially between an assertion and the meaning or sense which that assertion purports to convey. But surely that is just one step in the process?

Examples of truth assertion:

- 'it is raining in London'

The components of that statement being: (a) it is raining; (b) in; and (c) London.

Each of (a), (b) and (c) signifies something, and taken together, (a), (b) and (c) convey a particular message.

At this stage, we are in the realm of 'knowledge by definition'. We can be said to *know* (that is to say, understand) what it means to 'be raining', 'in' a location called 'London'.

Is it necessary to have at least experienced rainfall in order to know the sense of this assertion? I think not, because rather like the subject who asserts that 'orcas breed in the Atlantic', or the subject who has no sight but who states that 'this ball is spherical', the *experience* which these assertions purport to describe is not a necessary component of their meaning, nor is it necessary for someone to have had a particular experience for him or her to understand what each assertion means.

But being able to understand what an assertion *means* is just a preliminary step in the process of communication. Now that I understand what it means to say that 'it is raining in London', I also need to ensure that that assertion is not false.[6] There are various ways by which to do this. I can, for example, ask someone who is then in London, and who also understands the meaning of the assertion, to confirm its truth; or if I myself happen to be in London, and being outdoors I appear to be getting wet, and I am reminded that this is what happens when I stand in the midst of rainfall, then I can confirm this assertion for myself. In both cases, the participants in this process of communication must (a) understand what the assertion means, and (b) understand how the assertion is either confirmed or denied. It is not necessary, however, for the participants to demonstrate the correspondence between the assertion and some form of notional 'reality', nor is it necessary that this assertion forms a coherent matrix with any other assertion, save in the realm of linguistics (in particular, syntax).

Accordingly, apart from understanding the meanings of the words used and the composite meaning of the assertion, a participant who asserts that 'it is raining in London' must understand that location is a spatial term which necessarily concerns three-dimensional space; an

---

[6] Note that we are concerned here with truth and falsehood, not sense and nonsense. It is agreed that the assertion in this case is not nonsense.

Theories of Truth

event is a temporal term and concerns process; rain is a kind of 'substance', with a particular common feel and trajectory; and embedded in three-dimensional space are points or places which have been given specific names.[7]

I also need to know how assertions like this are confirmed or denied. I return then to the various ways by which the assertion may be confirmed or denied. Suppose I ask someone who is then situated in London, and he confirms that it is indeed raining around him. I can press him further and ask him how he has drawn that conclusion, and he might say that he can see what look to him like large droplets of a clear fluid falling earthwards, or *that*, and also that his clothes are wet, that the ink on the manuscript he is carrying is starting to 'run', and so on.

These are all signs or strategies which participants are or become familiar with, in order to confirm (or deny) that it is raining somewhere. In identifying and compiling these signs, and evoking these strategies, I do not need to demonstrate any form of correspondence between the assertion or its components and a purported reality. Nor does the assertion need to form part of a coherent matrix together with other assertions, save that the words that comprise, and the form of, the assertion, must be understood by each participant – in short, the participants must be consistent in their use of these words and the forms created therefrom; so that, if the assertion makes reference to 'rainfall', no participant conceives this (in

---

[7] But surely all that that concerns is the process of understanding the meanings of words and the composite meaning of this assertion!

error) to mean the sensation which results from touching a hard, cold, green substance.

If there is 'correspondence' here at all, it is correspondence between the components of and the whole sense of the assertion, and the various signs or strategies the participants utilise in order to confirm or deny (the truth of) the assertion. But even so, 'correspondence' is not the operative function. 'Rain' has the qualities x, y and z. Experiencing rainfall gives rise to a, b and c sensations. If our participant recognises qualities x, y and z as present, or experiences a, b and c sensations, then he or she is able to go some way towards confirming (the truth of) the assertion. Having done so, he or she can thereafter formulate (a representation of) reality, as it were. He or she will assert that (in reality) it is raining. So, in short, the correspondence is not one between the assertion and the aspect of 'reality' in question; rather, it is a *kind of* correspondence, for want of a better term, with the signs and strategies we use, which then enable us to formulate (or fabricate) a representation of 'reality'.

Both the 'qualities' and the 'sensations' in this matter provide the participant with a hook on which to hang the various parts of the assertion. Accordingly, rather than the 'picture of reality' or the 'model of the world', or somesuch, being key in this activity, the key 'correspondence' is between the parts of the assertion and individual perceptions.

Again, let us consider the assertion 'it is raining in London'. Both the speaker and his listeners will process this as follows:

1. The component 'it is raining' will elicit recollection of the sensation of rainfall and the assumption of immediacy;
2. The words 'in London' will elicit a recollection of a great deal of information (if I am in, or have been to, London, this may comprise recollections of my experiences there; if I have not, then recollections of impressions, experiences, historical and perhaps also pictorial data concerning London).

Which brings me to assertions made by participants who have no direct or personal experience of the subject matter of the assertion. Take for example 'the Burj Khalifa is the tallest building in Dubai', or 'the neutrino is a sub-atomic particle contained in the nucleus of an atom, with neither a positive nor a negative electrical charge'. If the speaker has had no personal experience of either subject matter – in short, if he or she has not with his or her own senses perceived either Dubai or the Burj, and certainly has not measured the building's height; and is ignorant of the structure of the atom, save through 'derived information' – then for that 'participant' this is either assumption or derived knowledge.

This leaves us with the following end result: the truth carrier 'it is now raining in London' asserts the following:

1. Assuming the truth of London;
2. Assuming an understanding of the terms 'now' and 'rain';
3. If an observer observes, or if it is observed, that 'rain', 'London', at the instant of observation;

4. The truth carrier 'it is now raining in London' is apparently confirmed.

What do we mean by 'truth' in the phrase 'the truth of London'? Or 'confirmed' in the sentence '"it is now raining in London" is apparently confirmed'? We need to understand our use of the word 'truth' as well as our use of 'confirmed' in order to know that we have indeed confirmed the truth carrier 'it is raining in London'.

The correspondence theory of truth is inapplicable to any truth carrier which does not concern a state of affairs or a fact.

Consider 'that vase is beautiful', or 'that vase is green', or 'it is wrong to kill [in any circumstances]', or 'I believe in free speech':

1. That vase is beautiful: p is a vase; I feel moved; I assume that p is a direct 'cause' of that feeling. Alternatively, p is a vase; p contains or exhibits w, b and a; w, b and a are individually or collectively 'qualities of beauty'.
2. That vase is green: p is a vase; I have direct knowledge of green; p is green.
3. p y, x (where 'y' is the act to kill); a states that y is n.
4. p y, x (where 'y' is the state of 'believing', and 'x' is a certain state of affairs).

Wittgenstein comments as follows: 'God does not reveal himself in the world'. That is a true statement in so far as nothing in the world is god itself (unless of course one is a pantheist). We conceive here of the 'world' and of 'god'.

We assert that neither the 'totality of the world', nor any of its parts, is what we mean by god; albeit that we may argue that 'god "made" the world'. But in so far as the world and the concept 'god' are distinct, the world is incapable of 'revealing' god; in short, there is no part or whole of god in the world.

Accordingly, statements about god are of a kind with statements about anything which is distinct from the world; for example, a counterfactual conditional such as 'if it rains, my umbrella will get wet', or statements which do not conform with the world such as: 'men and women are the direct descendants of beings who originated from Mars'.

As concerns the counterfactual, the statement it makes is by definition contrary to that which exists or is perceived, and therefore does not describe or refer to a fact. As concerns statements which do not conform with or to the world, the statement likewise does not describe the world, but rather something else.

- P believes that god exists
- God exists
- P is justified in believing that god exists

This is *not* equal to the assertion 'P believes that god exists because his mother told him so'. That is neither justification nor a good ground for his belief!

(B) Coherence

Why should 'coherence' in any manner be a necessary feature of truth or a truth function? It is a mere assumption on our parts that perceptions taken as a whole should in some sense 'cohere' with or support one another!

The difficulty lies in trying to understand what we mean by, or in what way we are using, the words 'coheres with' or 'corresponds with'. Coherence theories require the 'correspondence' to be between a proposition and [necessarily all] other propositions. By contrast, correspondence theories require a correspondence between the proposition or statement and facts or states of events.

As regards the correspondence theory, we do know what it would mean for a proposition to 'correspond with' a fact or facts.

I suggest that the coherence principle can be construed as follows: a proposition is true if (and only if) there is no other [true] proposition which contradicts it.

Typically, however, coherence theorists have said a proposition is true if it entails, or logically implies, or is consistent with, all other true propositions.

Note that 'truth is not "relative", in so far as something can be true for you but not for me'. Many of us may disagree with that assumption, arguing that truth is indeed relative to each 'observer'. But if 'truth' (however that is described) were *in every instance* relative to each 'observer', then chaos would ensue. It is principally the degree of uniformity or 'sameness' which *most* observed phenomena, and the tools we utilise to make our observations, appear to have, which enables 'observers' to communicate their observations to one another.

Coherence theories present us with the difficulty that we may well be able to ascertain whether any one proposition is coherent with other true propositions, or is not contradicted by any one or more true propositions; but how can we know whether any purportedly 'true' proposition *is true*? There is a great deal written on the coherence theory of truth, and the curious reader may do well to spend some time familiarising themselves with that literature.

Focusing only on propositions, statements or sentences is too restrictive an activity, because the greater part of our 'picture of the world' or of 'reality' or the state of things, is provided by virtue of the various 'messages' received through our sense organs – primarily our eyes and ears – but also, crucially, our capacity to sense through touch. Any language which aims to portray 'reality', must work consistently with the stimuli we receive through our sense organs.

Take the following propositions or statements:

- 'Alexander was a Macedonian'
- 'the sky is [or 'looks'] grey [today]'

Propositions or statements (of fact) must correspond *not* with 'reality', as it were, but with the stimuli received by our sense organs; accordingly, there is only one way to demonstrate the correctness of the statement 'the sky is grey', and that is to observe the sky (or for someone to observe the sky on our behalf).

Even the truth or falsehood of a complex historical statement, such as 'Alexander was a Macedonian', is demonstrated by way of a large amount of information received primarily by our eyes, in the form of documentary and physical evidence. Move from this to a present day event. Imagine a statement about present matters such as 'Edward owns a cottage in Provence'. This is easily demonstrated by way of visual data concerning an individual called 'Edward' and a 'cottage in Provence'. Ownership may be demonstrated by virtue of a deed of title or the equivalent.

To posit 'reality' is therefore unnecessary, and it is an assumption which we need not make. 'Reality' may indeed be construed as a shorthand for 'the stimuli [an individual] receives from various sense organs, which he or she then gives cognitive form'.

It is important for us to bear in mind that not *all* 'propositions', as propositions rather than statements, affirmations or the like, are or can be 'reduced to language'.

For example, many, if not most, of our visual and auditory stimuli have a 'pre-linguistic' form. When I look at the sky or hear a bird song, I am not necessarily thinking of a statement such as 'the sky is [or looks] grey', or 'I hear a bird's warble', but even prior to any such thought which has linguistic form, the stimulus may be said to take the form of a proposition – something descriptive, the 'truth' of which can be demonstrated or refuted.

If other observers can see a blue sky instead, then there is a probability (say) that my pre-linguistic experience, resulting in the proposition 'the sky is [or looks] grey', is false, as is the linguistic form of that pre-linguistic experience. If it can be shown that there are no birds around me, my perceiving a warble, which I took to be a bird's warble, is incorrect or inaccurate, or perhaps even wholly delusionary.

Propositions can and frequently do exist in a pre-linguistic form, and their truth or falsehood is always the subject of determination. So much for the objects of perception. It is not difficult to see that such objects are or can be each given a truth function.

But as for the numerous other types of 'proposition' which do not have an apparent or obvious connection with perceived data, is there any point in also considering their truth value? Necessarily, the kinds of proposition in this instance will in every case be verbal in form; we are talking about such propositions as beliefs, opinions or analyses.

A statement such as 'god loves you' is certainly *prima facie* capable of being conceived as a truth-bearing proposition. On a simplistic level, if it can be shown that god in fact does not love you, then the statement is false; if it can be shown that 'god', as we have defined it for the purposes of this particular statement, does not 'exist' (i.e. there is no corresponding 'reality' which the word refers to), then the statement is false (not nonsensical).

We should try to distinguish between nonsensical and false statements. A false statement is perhaps capable of describing 'reality', but allegedly does not 'correspond' with that 'reality'. A nonsensical statement can never correspond with reality. Some statements are both nonsensical and false, for example, a false statement about an event in the past.

Likewise, my statement that 'the sky is [or looks] grey' is not nonsensical (in the same sense as my statement 'god loves you'), but if it can be shown (necessarily by way of observation, because a colour is necessarily observed through or with the eyes) that the sky is 'blue' or, more accurately, 'looks blue' to (let us say) a number of observers, then my statement is shown to be false; we would hardly say instead that my statement is nonsensical, if only because it is capable of being shown to be true or false.

But one might argue that the statement 'god loves you', is *not* capable of being shown to be either true or false; that it has the same form as any other belief;

[Is it the case that any belief is by definition incapable of being shown to be either true or false?]

Description, Explanation and Meaning

What is 'meaning'? I suggest that the word applies only to language or linguistic utterances, in the broadest of senses.

We are concerned here with symbolic form which 'stands for' or 'represents' something else besides that symbolic form itself. Therefore, the symbolic form

means a form of sound or a sound with a particular quality or form; the word 'frog' means, or is a reference to, a certain kind of perceived creature. But the frog itself, the creature, is devoid of any 'meaning'. As a consequence, it is nonsense to talk about perceived phenomena as having 'meaning' – they are what they are, and that is all.

What of 'explanation'? It is possible to explain a perceived phenomenon, and that is precisely what we do when we say that rust which has formed on the surface of an iron object is the result of a [chemical] combination of certain elements – iron, oxygen and the like. Or that the flood that took the lives of hundreds of people was the result of spiritual forces, or the displeasure of the gods, or even an unseasonal deluge of precipitation.

Can we say that the flood has 'meaning'? I can *describe* the flood as, for example, having X source or Y trajectory, or a certain approximate volume of water or speed of flow, and so on. But I cannot *explain* the flood, nor can I find any meaning in it as an event.

It is incorrect, therefore, to speak of perceptible events as having meaning. We say, for example, 'his death was without meaning', which is to say that his death was something of a 'waste', which is to say that if someone were to die, there should be a 'purpose', an 'underlying purpose' or 'meaning' to the death.

That is a clear misuse of the word 'meaning'. What we really intend to say is that that event must have 'significance', or at the very minimum be a means to a certain end. In this case, the death seemed to be *sans* significance, and no particular 'end' was served by it. But the death itself has neither meaning, nor is it meaningless.

The symbol π on the other hand, has a meaning in mathematics; it represents a certain numerical value. Accordingly, it is possible to say that π as a mathematical symbol means (or represents) the value 3.142.

Description, or the process of describing something, is distinguishable from the ascription of meaning to something; albeit that *meaning* is given to a certain symbolic form, and it is also possible to describe that particular

Description, Explanation and Meaning

symbolic form. I can write the Greek letter π, describing this as a symbol comprising two short parallel vertical lines, joined at their apex by a short wavy horizontal line, or as the nth letter in the Greek alphabet; and I can also say that 'π' in mathematics 'stands for', or *means*, the numerical value 3.142.

Physical phenomena, however, whatever form they may take, do not have meaning; at least not in the sense that I have used this term. Though I may say that the death of Mahatma Gandhi was a moment 'pregnant with meaning', what I really mean is that his death is or was of great significance or import (or more simply, that his death was regrettable); but not that that singular event *means* anything, as though it were a symbol representing something else.

Take another example – that of our propensity to (misdescribe) certain kinds of phenomena. We have heard it said that certain individuals can do very odd things with ordinary phenomena. It has been reported that certain individuals have caused dust to 'turn into' living things. This tells us nothing about the phenomena themselves, save that it appears that dust has 'turned into' life form, say; but nor does this tell us anything very definitive about the person who performs these marvels, save that that person appears to have a capability very uncommon among people.

On Revelation

If a non-sensory revelation, that is to say, an 'experience' of something extra-mundane, call it 'spiritual', does indeed manifest itself to some of us, where lies the rationale behind the belief that any one revelation is either exclusive or true? Which begs the further question, by what means can we discover the truth? Which itself begs the question, what do we mean by truth? Which in turn begs the question, how do we construe of falsehood, or more precisely, how do we distinguish between truth and falsehood? Assuming the veracity of a revelation, how is it possible to decide its meaning, separate from its significance? Does a perception contain 'meaning'? If not, then why should one suppose that a revelation (assuming that it is a species of perception) contains meaning?

A revelation of this kind is problematical on two grounds: first, it is typically incapable of confirmation or denial, as an event; and second, it is conceived as more than just an event – it is apparently a special species of event which itself has meaning, just as any other symbolical form has meaning.

On Revelation

Let us assume that a 'miracle' is an event which appears to be contrary to 'ordinary experience'.[8] Even if a miracle could be shown to have occurred,[9] it is illegitimate to assume therefore that the event is anything more than the event itself. What leads us to suppose that the event can demonstrate the existence of an extra-mundane reality? Isn't that extra-mundane reality similar to the 'theoretical' component in the physical sciences – after all, who has seen a 'quark' or a 'neutrino'?[10] Let us imagine a situation in which a man takes hold of a handful of dust, and the dust 'turns into' a bird. That is utterly incapable, in itself, of demonstrating anything but the fact itself. Facts, after all, do not themselves contain meaning. They simply subsist, as it were.

Let us revert for a moment to truth and falsehood. Though we have devised a number of strategies pursuant to which we decide between truth and falsehood, these strategies are appropriate only to either mundane things or to abstract concepts.

---

[8] Notice that for an event to comprise a *miraculous* event, it must be extra-ordinary, so that ordinary events (in short, events which occur regularly and are therefore commonplace) cannot be construed of as miraculous. There is no clear reason as to why this should be the case, save that the assumption appears to be that deities participate in the events of the phenomenal world only occasionally. Curiously, that the extra-ordinary and therefore infrequent nature of an "act of God", so to speak, is a defining feature, has even found its way into the legal concept *force majeure*!

[9] In short, it can be demonstrated that the event itself has indeed occurred.

[10] That said, it is not my intention to assert that explaining an event as having an 'extra-mundane' cause, is in any sense materially similar to explaining an event as being caused by a possible sub-atomic particle.

Repetition or regularity is one such strategy, and verification is another. Tests may be devised in order to demonstrate, as best we can, a particular circumstance. No such strategy can be applied to an event which will not, and indeed cannot by definition, occur more than once. Any such event is therefore likely to be incapable of being subjected to tests of any kind.

But even if the event itself was unique, or in other words, incapable of repetition, it is impossible to demonstrate that the event was evidence of, or (more dubiously) signified, an extra-mundane reality.[11] The dust in the subject's hands can arguably be shown to be dust, subjected to analysis and so on. The bird which thereafter appears can also arguably be shown to be just a bird, and subjected to whatever analysis we wish to devise. But none of this can demonstrate anything, save that the subject has apparently handled dust and 'created' a bird (arguably) therefrom. We may have no means of explaining that transition – from dust to bird – and as a result, *some* observers may conclude that the event signifies (for example) an extra-mundane reality. But it is noteworthy that firstly, we are not *bound* to draw the same conclusion as those observers (the conclusion does not follow from the event itself); and secondly, an event does not signify anything – it does not contain 'meaning'.

---

[11] We might also argue, with some force, that the words 'extra-mundane reality' contain a contradiction in terms!

An Essay on Epistemology

Knowledge may concern or be described as either (a) a sensory perception, or an inference drawn from a sensory perception, or (b) a thought process or a proposition, without reference or apparently without reference to a prior sensory perception.

Though it may be stretching the meaning of the word 'knowledge', an example of item (b) above is fantasy; but it remains nevertheless possible to draw a parallel between fantasy and one or more sensory perceptions, at least in so far as that which is imagined bears similarity to that which has been or can be perceived. What is questionable, however, is to what extent 'fantasy' can be construed as knowledge, as defined.

What of hallucination? In so far as it can be demonstrated that that which was perceived or apparently perceived by one or more individuals was or could not be generally perceived, we relegate that perception or apparent perception to the realms of hallucination. We presuppose, therefore, that (a) a perception, in order to be a perception, must at least be capable of 'general observation', and (b) a perception must be necessarily *about* something, the truth (or falsehood) of which should be demonstrable.

A hallucination can therefore fall within the category of a perception in so far as it may be *about* something, the truth or falsehood of which can be demonstrated, or is at least capable of demonstration; but a hallucination, by definition, cannot be capable of general observation, as a perception can. *[But consider mass hallucination. It is arguable that mass hallucination, though it appears to involve the perception of something identifiable, by more than one percipient, is incapable of general observation]*

We therefore distinguish between that which is capable of general observation and that which is not. If something is not capable of general observation then we dismiss the purported observation as being a chimera. But that, merely, is how we define a perception. It must be capable of general observation that is to say observation by more than one percipient. What if a percipient were to be able to make the same or similar observation on more than one occasion, but no other percipient were capable of or able to make that observation? Would that be sufficient to constitute a perception? There is no reason, in principle, why such an observation or purported observation could not be construed of as a perception. One cannot argue that, *a priori*, an observation made by a percipient, but not by any other percipient, is not capable of being a perception. But that would be impractical. If only one percipient were capable of observing something, and no other percipient were capable of doing so, that observation would appear to be of little epistemological value. If only I myself were capable of an observation (and I stress that the point is that only one percipient should be *capable* of that observation), and it were not possible in the sense that no other percipient could be capable of that observation, it is conceivable that that observation has an epistemological value for me, but surely it is of doubtful value for any other percipient.

Accordingly, though it is conceivable that only a single percipient may be capable of a particular observation, it may nevertheless be argued that that observation is a perception, as defined.

The words 'general observation', therefore, would appear to be with two possible meanings. First, that it should be capable of observation by more than one percipient (though it is the subject of further analysis as to how one can ascertain whether the observation of each percipient is 'alike'); and second, that it should be capable of being observed more than once by the same percipient. But this latter limb appears to be illegitimate. Why could it not be said that an observation by a percipient made only once, and no more than that, is capable of being construed as a perception? It is conceivable that that single observation can be construed of as a perception, and in some manner have epistemological value for the percipient in question. Yes, conceivable, but of limited or no efficacy; just as it is conceivable that only one of us is *capable* of perceiving something, but any such purported perception is of doubtful efficacy!

In any event, suppose it were argued that it is not the epistemological value of a perception which is the defining feature of that perception; that a perception can be a perception *sans* any epistemological value. That depends on how we construe epistemological value. Can it not be said that any observation made is capable of having epistemological value, at least for the percipient?

Let's return for a moment to the subject of hallucination. I suggest that there are very few people who would want to argue that a hallucination comprises knowledge, as I have described this; and indeed most of us might consider it perverse to grant a hallucination the exalted status of knowledge. Most of us would argue that a hallucination should not be construed as knowledge merely because it is not a 'representation of things as they actually are', or somesuch. The same can be said for 'fantasy'. As a consequence, I would argue that fantasy too, like hallucination, should not be construed to be a form or instance of knowledge.

So, it seems that knowledge should possess a status different from that of fantasy or hallucination.

What causes me a degree of discomfort, though, is the understanding that although fantasy can quite readily be shown to have no direct connection with a perceived 'reality' so that there is no need to try to confirm or deny the veracity of a fantasy in whatever form that takes, but hallucination does indeed share a number of the key features of the kind of perception which we would describe as an instance of 'knowledge'.

An Essay on Time

Time may indeed 'exist' in the absence of 'motion', but in the absence of 'motion', time cannot be measured, and therefore loses any significance.

Motion may include thought processes, and a thought process can manifest itself in a number of ways: a number of separate or distinct perceptions; stimuli such as change in temperature; or language, a process in the form of words.

If in the absence of motion, time is not capable of measurement, is it legitimate to say that 'time passes'? Is time therefore anything more than the sensation of motion, or does time have an 'existence' separate from motion?

Consider a universe comprising composition, be it uniform or varied. That universe necessarily occupies 'space'. Is it legitimate to say that any one point in that spatial universe has a different time value from that of any other point in that universe?

Consider a vacuum with a spatial dimension. Is it legitimate to say that any one point in that vacuum has a different time value to that of any other point in that vacuum? Certainly it is conceivable that that is the case, but time has a pragmatic function. It enables a perceiver to comprehend and manage perceptible space. In the absence of perceptible space, time loses its value.

-2-

Theoretical physicists claim that it is possible to 'travel' backwards in time.

Their supposition has its basis in a fallacy, namely the conception that matter continues to exist in the past, as it were. The fallacy lies also in the assumption of parallel universes.

The fallacies of time travel and parallel universes are counter-intuitive, and contrary to [ordinary] experience.

On 1 July, in any one year, 30 June has ceased to exist. The concept of time travel is based on a fallacious sense of an unbroken continuum of matter, straddling both 30 June and 1 July; so that one can move back and forth along that continuum, as though on a track enabling movement in two opposite directions.

Accordingly, one could never conceivably return to one's own past, or travel to one's own future. Though travelling to a future time does seem to be conceptually possible.

Is it conceivable for an individual to travel to another individual's future time?

On the Limits of Logic

1. Time and space appear to be infinite.

2. The dimensions of the universe are therefore apparently without border or shape.

3. Indeed, it appears that the universe has no dimensions.

4. Likewise, number is in principle capable of infinity.

5. Mind, however, and therefore the concepts which act as the basis of human language, has discrete boundaries.

6. The mind is incapable of conceiving of infinite number or infinite space.

7. The mind is incapable of conceiving that which may lie beyond the perceivable universe.

8. All that can be conceived is at least based on all that is perceived.

PART II

No… No, Let's Throw Logic and Good Reason to the Wind!

On Institutionalised Religion

What do I mean by institutionalised religion? For purposes of this discourse, institutionalised religion comprises popular religious or theological dogma which by its nature does not concern itself with its own veracity, has no time for idle introspection or self-doubt, and attempts to be systematic in its treatment of that religion, so as to present it to the public as though it were of one defined body.

By contrast, religious or theological thought, in the absence of religious or theological dogma or institutionalised religion, is prone to self-doubt, though where such thought is itself embedded in or grows from the structure of religious or theological dogma, that dogma can be developed further; though this endeavour being what it is, unless such thought is in some manner imbued with a spiritual dimension (and how one ascertains this is difficult for me to conceive), such thought can be no more than an intellectual endeavour.

And spirituality, in the absence of religious or theological thought, is mere babble without sense.

That said, we are obliged to conceive of the spiritual

dimension by its very terminology as being 'other than' the physical dimension, and indeed 'dimensions' themselves are an abstract or solipsistic means of coping with essentially different phenomena; the one being concerned with the perceptible universe, *sans* the spiritual dimension, and the other being concerned with either the less easily explicable range of our perceptions or with the logical, or apparently logical, consequences of pure thought. But it is difficult to understand in what sense or by way of what processes of thought, the precepts of morality (let us assume that these are universal) "present to us with an inexplicable authority". That, surely, remains squarely within the confines of the mind and language. Notwithstanding, if God, freedom and immortality are the necessary consequences of the moral law, then they are merely the logically necessary consequences of the moral law, a supposition which is incapable of being tested by whatever means ordinarily available to us. And though it may be argued by some that it is possible to intuitively derive mystical knowledge which is capable of analysis and expression, it is difficult to square such intuitions with our ordinary range of perceptions.

But be that as it may, the conceptual difficulties which institutional religious thinking sets before us are a concern, as one of the broader consequences of these difficulties is that institutional religion does not seem to have efficacy. The ordinary believer being what he is, he can neither cope with even the logical consequences of religious thought, nor can he translate that religious thought into his daily affairs. As a consequence, the ordinary believer works merely on the plane of a collection of mantras which he has been led to believe, and which he believes without question, save when he suffers moments of doubt. In many cases, thankfully, such moments of doubt are transitory, and the ordinary believer, such as he is, will resume his beliefs without much modification of his earlier state of knowledge, but with a dogged acceptance that that which he suffered was either that which he was fated to suffer, or that it was in some manner salutary. Of course, confused thinking such as this is not unique to religious discourse, but I suggest that the significance of the confusion is potentially far more dangerous and wide-reaching in a religious context than it is in any other. What concerns me, then, is the fallibility of the ordinary believer, who believes but does not (and probably cannot) understand that which he believes.

No matter how sophisticated the believer, there remains much in institutional religion which makes little or no sense as a metaphysical or epistemological medium. It may indeed be the case that God, freedom and immortality are the logical consequences of the moral law, but our knowledge of God, assuming that that knowledge is not merely a logical consequence of the moral law but is also the result of momentary revelation, is tainted.

If the moral law and revelation also causes us to conceive of God as good, or better still, of *the* good, or the ultimate good, whatever that is, then we must struggle to make sense of that which is the absence of good, or worse still, what we mortals term 'evil'. Our more significant institutional religions have gone some way towards making sense of that term. As an example, the Christian religion has itself developed over time, and many of its more significant developments are the result of a mix of argument, contemplation and occasional revelation.

It should not surprise us therefore that the body of beliefs it presents us with are rarely capable of systematic treatment. We have looked briefly at two of the dominant theories of truth – it appears that neither of these theories is a happy bedfellow with religious discourse. Most systematic thought will at least sometimes be guilty of nonsense or self-contradiction. In some instances, these difficulties affect areas which are central to that 'system'.

As a principal question, let us ask ourselves if there is a nexus between a "good" act and a "bad" 'consequence'. If there is, we have the basis for a system of ethics. But in order to be a 'system' as such (in short, in order to achieve a degree of coherence), the consequences of an action must surely be consistently applied – it is not satisfactory if in some cases the consequence of a good act is a bad consequence. It is not enough to argue that this is because, perhaps try as we may, that which we can achieve in the way of "goodness" falls short of that which is required of us to necessitate a "good" consequence; does that explain why our lives are invariably a mix of both good and bad consequences? It is not satisfactory to argue that we have misunderstood the nature of good and bad, because in that event, there is a clear risk that we may have also misunderstood the nature of the ultimate good.

It is not good enough to argue that perhaps we have misunderstood the ultimate good, in as far as the consequences we expect to arise from our better deeds are not within the scope of his activities. Or, though God is good, he is either unwilling or unable to match good deeds with good consequences and bad deeds with bad consequences. Or that good deeds are "rewarded" with good consequences only at some later time, for example, in the afterlife. But once again, that fails to explain why in the case of some good deeds, we appear to experience consequential good effects, but in the case of other good deeds, we do not. We are all endowed with a comparatively limited understanding of the various experiences we each have; in order to understand those experiences, we rely very much on our faculties, which appear to function in a specified and restricted manner. It is really not good enough if we are asked to be selective in the operation of or reliance on these faculties!

What is God?

By its definition, almost, a god must be that which is not the perceptible world, for if the perceptible world were itself god, then it would be nothing more than the perceptible world itself. And in the same way, a carrot cannot be a beetroot. But instead, we speak of god, be it pantheistic or otherwise, as though it were an essence which is other than the perceptible world. Nor can it be correct to say that god can be identified with man, for (without wishing to play mere games of nomenclature) man is most clearly far from divine in character!

There is, however, a tendency in most men to imagine a state of divinity. And god has been fashioned by some as though it were personal or endowed with a persona, acting in very much the same manner as would man itself, but without form or substance; and by others, as though it were some ethereal or imperceptible aspect of the phenomenal world itself. Either separate from, albeit responsible for, the phenomenal world, or an aspect of the phenomenal world. Either personal, or impersonal.

Whichever form we give consideration to, it is

disappointing that neither our ability to perceive the phenomenal world nor our ability to conceive of or 'experience' the apparently supra- or non-phenomenal can assist us to 'touch' god, as we quite clearly can touch a stone, and feel its size, its colour, shape and consistency. We touch the stone, and though we may well be deluded as to its presence, or some might say, as to its true presence, we appear to recognise a relationship, apparently a logical relationship, between our perceptible actions in handling the stone and the perceptible consequences of our handling of the stone. There is no such relationship, and seldom a logical relationship, between our supposed conversations with god, or more dubiously, our 'dealings' with god on a phenomenal level, and any perceptible consequences of that conversation or those dealings. It is surely easy enough to suppose that those consequences, if they exist, are solely conceptual, given our propensity to delude ourselves as to the veracity of unaided thought. By unaided thought, I refer to thought with no apparent causal nexus with the phenomenal world. I may think of 'rain', but if it is not then raining anywhere around me, it is a thought with no apparent causal nexus with the phenomenon of rain (except either in the form of the recollection of an event, or of acquired knowledge). Similarly, I may conceive of a spiritual presence in my midst (I do not think that we can say that I perceive that presence as I perceive a stone, so let us not delude ourselves into talking of this as though it were a perception), but try as I might, I am singularly unable to 'deal' with that presence, as I deal with a stone.

Notwithstanding that almost total absence of the

ability to 'deal' with the spiritual 'realm', there are those of us who appear to believe in its existence. It cannot be described; indeed, if one were to try to describe that realm, one could do so only with the language of perceptible experience. Notwithstanding, one holds steadfastly to that belief. And yet, if I were to step outdoors with my umbrella open, then look at my umbrella and, perceiving it to be dry, were to tell my neighbour that it must surely be raining, how might he reply?

For this reason alone, if our god was with persona, we would run into frequent difficulty when attempting to 'deal' with that persona.

On the other hand, if that god were no more nor less than the perceptible universe in some form, our 'dealings' with that perceptible universe are no less likely to enable us to perceive god, as they enable us merely to perceive the perceptible universe.

What causes me some difficulty is this. We learn to construe the perceptible world around us through an understanding of causality. The building blocks of classical modern science appeared to have their basis in our understanding of causality. But what of 'god'? Where lies the causality in his actions? Is he not instead the very embodiment, if embodiment be the permissible word in this case, of free will? And what does that mean? That that which has free will, in its fullest sense, acts in an extra-causal manner, is untouched by causality; is frivolous, capricious, and does as it pleases. And yet, the Christian God is imbued not just with absolute free will, but is also bound up with the world of causality. He is capricious in the fullest sense of the word, and yet he can be controlled. I can describe his actions in a conditional mode. If I do thus, the consequences of my action are inevitably so.

Is that such an issue after all? Perhaps it is. For as long as we imbue godhead with such absolutes as absolute freedom of will, we fall into difficulty when we grant that same godhead an antithetical quality, albeit that that antithetical quality is not itself an absolute. And so, a god who has absolute free will must, so our various revelations tell us, on occasions act in accordance with specific events. If god is absolute goodness, (more so, if he and he alone is *the* good), he cannot also be its antithesis, at least not in so far as we apply the simplest of rules of logic to our description of his godhead. Perhaps in answer to our confusion, we might consider abandoning the rules of logic and throw the restrictions of language to the wind, and conceive instead of godhead as being nothing less than everything! But that is hardly a sensible conclusion to draw.

Let us consider a commonly conceived scenario in the established religions. For that purpose, let me restrict the enquiry to Christian dogma. Let us commence the enquiry by stating that god has ultimate free will. What do we mean by that? Though it is a concept impossible to define with any precision, let us assume that what that means is that god will not be fettered. He does as he pleases and is not confined to the limitations of causality. In short, in the realm of causality, we begin with the formula 'if X then Y', but for a presence which can act and yet act contrary to the confines of causality, the formula would appear to be 'if X, then an infinite range of consequences', or more conceivably, 'if X, then Y or not Y', or 'if X, then one of a number of conceivable consequences'. Let us breathe life into that formula. A sufferer prays hard for deliverance from his sufferings. He is truly contrite. He is very much in touch with his Deliverer. But his Deliverer need not respond in accordance with those prayers. He may, and yet he may not. And so the consequences of speaking to one's Deliverer do not bear much similarity to the consequences of 'religiously' treating an illness with the appropriate "medicaments". As a result, just as our fortunes are very much like the consequences of a lottery, so too is the Deliverer's response to the pleadings of his loyal subject.

But let us suppose, instead, that we have misunderstood both the nature as well as the character of the Deliverer. Let us imagine instead that there is indeed a logic to the concept of indulgences! Let us suppose that he inexorably acts within the confines of causality. What evidence do we have that that is indeed the case? Very little, it seems.

We could argue that the perceptible world – indeed, the only world we appear to know and inhabit – is illusory and the illusions are, in any event, passing. We could argue that the consequences of the sufferer's pleadings are not perceptible, and cannot be perceived as we perceive a stone. We could argue that passing through this illusory world, our sufferer will then "perceive" the Deliverer and/or "perceive" the (just?) consequences of his pleadings. In short, that the Deliverer does indeed act within the confines of some supra-phenomenal causality, but the separation of realms being such as it is – phenomenal, as separate from the supra-phenomenal – we do not, and will not, perceive the consequences of the sufferer's prayers until we 'perceive', or by virtue of our experience of that supra-phenomenal realm.

On the other hand, in attempting to describe the character of the Deliverer, one could, throwing aside the science of causality entirely, argue that the Deliverer is indeed capricious and has free 'will' in the sense that the Deliverer does not act consequentially, but instead, contra-consequentially. That might mean that the Deliverer's acts are inexplicable as logical consequences of the acts of the sufferer. That might be a little short of saying that that which is a logical consequence of the sufferer's prayer is precisely that which the Deliverer will not do. But that, surely, runs counter to the Christian concept of the Deliverer, and must surely therefore be abandoned.

These conceptual problems, I imagine, are undoubtedly the result of difficulties relating to the concepts themselves. Let us talk in terms not of freedom of will, but instead of unfettered choice, by which we mean infinite choice. Let us imagine that whereas man's choice is fettered by the limited number of choices he has available to choose from – and it is conceivable that in a number of instances (or arguably even many, or perhaps even all instances), he will have just the one choice – by contrast, god's ability to choose is not so fettered.

In an ethical framework, then (taking only the Judaeo-Christian framework as an illustration), it is supposed that god is free to punish or to reward an individual as he 'wishes', so to speak. Bear in mind, too, that when we talk of god's free will (in the Judaeo-Christian framework), we are necessarily talking of god's free will in an ethical context, rather than in a metaphysical sense. He shall not be fettered; and yet, if one takes that argument to its logical conclusion, though it may indeed be highly probable that as a consequence of my act he will punish me, he will (being of unfettered will) retain the capacity (so to speak) to do otherwise.

And so it appears that god's free will means nothing short of the capacity to act capriciously. To draw that conclusion, however, is both ethically unsatisfactory and dissatisfying. If one cannot, in fact, depend (as it were) on god's punishment in circumstances where it is justified (justified according to his own ethical framework) – indeed, if there are circumstances in which god (acting capriciously) responds either by doing nothing, or more strangely still, by rewarding that malfeasance – then god is indeed capable of being capricious and unfettered, even by his own ethical framework.

Take another issue: if we hold something and it causes us pain, we recoil, and avoid further contact with it. But on the contrary, our interaction with that which we conceive of as divinity is not so determined. We assert the omnipotence as well as the mercy of our divine presence, and yet suffering harm, we blame ourselves and remain steadfast to our belief both in his presence, and also in his continuing benevolence. The truth must therefore be that epistemology differs markedly from religious sentiment.

Whichever way one looks at the matter, one appears to meet with difficulty. If one seeks an explanation for his failure to alleviate our pain, we face one or other of a number of intractable conclusions. Can it be because he is not in fact fully empowered, and we are wrong in supposing that, first, the divinity has the qualities of sentiment and compassion, and second, that he is empowered to act? But that or these are essential qualities which some of us ascribe to him, which he does not possess. Can it be that he lacks mercy? Again, one presumes that the divinity has sentiment and compassion, but the truth may be otherwise, if divinity there be. Could it be that he is not, or not fully, of this world, and to that degree, is incapable of influencing it, or if capable of doing so, is indifferent to doing so? In any event, the supposition that there is a "world" which is not *this* one is hardly something a rational individual ought to try to maintain. Could it be that he is unaware of human pain? Then that too would be to divorce him of a quality we consider to be crucial to his divinity.

Taken in the round, it is possible that we are led into difficulty precisely because we try to conceive of the divinity as though it were human, with many of the qualities possessed by us. Indeed, the Judaeo-Christian concept of divinity relies on the belief that we men are ourselves "made in his image", by which one is led to suppose that certain qualities we possess are inherited qualities, as it were, and are also qualities possessed by the divinity, but in some non-temporal and purer form. Mercy or compassion, for example; goodness and even knowledge being others.

Even the oldest monotheistic religion (arguably also the most uncluttered by cultural change and quasi-philosophical argument), namely Zoroastrianism[12], appears to lead us to the same errors. Though the Zoroastrian divinity is perhaps less likely to cause us conceptual confusion, in so far as it is not (as far as I am aware) a personality, or endowed with personality, and nor is it (at least for the present time) of infinite power, it contains all the above qualities of humanity. However, the Zoroastrian divinity, not being in possession of infinite power, does not always "conquer" that which it acts in opposition to; or to put this differently, the effect which that "opposite" tendency has on human actions is not in every case neutralised and thereafter superseded by the effect which that divinity has on us. To that extent, one appears to be better able to provide an explanation as to why on the one hand, the god of the Zoroastrians *exists*, but on the other, why men and women repeatedly fail to do that which is "good".

It is obvious that these illogicalities are very probably the result of the limitations not merely of the human mind, but also of human language. Our minds are capable of comprehending only so much, and in only such and such a manner, and human language is capable of describing human experience or abstract matters utilising only the linguistic parameters of that language – the more "primitive" the language, the less capable it may be of describing either experience or abstraction with any degree of veracity. That, of course, pre-supposes that the truth is itself necessarily complex, and yet it may not be.

---

[12] It is noteworthy that the Zoroastrian faith has had a strong influence on the development of Judaism and its own belief system.

Notwithstanding, given that our direct and commonplace experiences (whatever the nature of one's mind or the qualities of one's language be) are seldom, if ever, about divinity, why is it that we feel the need to describe one's experiences in relation to divinity?

Of course, none of us is capable of understanding every aspect of experience. So confusion, albeit occasional for some of us, may leave us with a desire for answers, so to speak. It is crucial, surely, that we are *consistent* in the manner in which we seek answers. It is crucial also that our 'answers', such as they are, are consistent with experience; and that our answers, such as they are, form something of a 'body' of belief – in short, that there is consistency between its many 'parts', just as any body should have, if it is to function appropriately! It is also crucial that we are generally prepared to abandon any 'part' which appears *inconsistent* either with our broad experience, or with the other parts of that system of belief.

So it appears that religious discourse and religious thinking flouts too many of the fundamental principles of either the way we receive and process information, or the way we develop any other body of information. Admittedly, we do not have a clear understanding of every element of experience. Take as one's starting point the human species itself, and as one watches it in its myriad activities, we can grow uneasy and feel little else but disdain for its crass stupidity, its greed, its capacity for hatred, its immense and unjustifiable pride; yes, we *can* as a consequence, either feel forced to withdraw from any further contact with this ill-conceived but self-possessed organism, or we may be tempted to seek excuses for its fallibility and folly. When we witness the great cruelty humankind is capable of, we may be tempted to conceive of just such a species but with a capacity for immeasurable kindness; witnessing the foolishness with which this species conducts its affairs, we may be led to conceive of a state of infinite wisdom; witnessing the hatred or the scorn with which men treat not just each other but also the world at large, we may be drawn to feel that there must exist a state of infinite love. And what is such infinite love or infinite wisdom, but the wretched state which we find ourselves in, *sans* the taint of our very existence – our immodesty, our utter failure to achieve anything but the basest of sentiments, try as we might?

So we draw the conclusion that the world cannot, therefore, be populated merely with such foolish and inhospitable creatures whose greatest failing appears to be that they have learned the art of self-justification! Ah, but the conclusion does *not* follow from the premise!

Further, though it does not appear to be possible to deal with the spiritual as one might be able to perceive of oneself dealing with the phenomenal world, for some of us it appears that the spirit has content, for there are events in our lives which require description or are more fully described through the language not just of perceptible content but of something else besides, and we are discomfited by the fact that the language that we use to describe the phenomenal world is inadequate to describe these other matters. I do not refer here to miraculous events, or to phenomena which are perceptible but inexplicable in terms of common parlance. Rather, I refer to perceptible events in our lives which appear to bear a dimension separate or distinct from the perceptible, which other dimension enables us to better comprehend or 'give meaning to' that perception. To illustrate, I take the commonplace example of human suffering. It is said that human suffering has both ultimate purpose, that is to say there is a 'reason' for which we suffer, and also a *function*, which one might call an epistemological function, as it acts as a guide to our future conduct.

Looking, first, at the epistemological function of human suffering, one would suppose that a necessary consequence of the experience of one's own suffering would be to withdraw from or avoid events which appear to be the direct cause of such suffering. If, on the contrary, we are enjoined to greet such suffering with a welcome, that must be because we conceive of an ultimate purpose and a function for human suffering which is ulterior to commonplace human experience. For how else can we explain the belief that human suffering is itself a mere means, a pathway, towards an end which itself is contra-phenomenal, or at least *extra*-phenomenal?

As to the ultimate purpose of human suffering, I see no distinction between suffering as it is experienced by man, and suffering as it is experienced by any other life form. Though the exact qualities of each of these forms of suffering may sometimes differ, just as it is hard to comprehend a *purpose* underlying the suffering of a dying animal, say, so it is also foolish (in my opinion) to envisage a *purpose* to human suffering. The purpose, in any event, is *not* a necessary component of that experience, so let us not pretend that such purpose exists.

It is curious also that religions (or religious thought) in every case appear to be the 'observations' of a particular individual or a particular group within a particular society. These 'observations' are not, therefore, the 'observations' of *any* observer or of all (possible) observers, but of a *particular* observer or observers in a *particular* context. It is hard to give observations such as these, which appear to be in every case 'partisan', the status of 'knowledge'. An 'observation' which comprises knowledge should, after all, be at least in principle an 'observation' which any observer should be capable of.

If, on the contrary, we argue that considerations such as these *can* only be revealed to a few of us, I am forced to ask the simple question 'why?' What is it about 'observations' such as this, which require, a particular set of faculties to conceive or perceive? What do these 'particular' kinds of faculty comprise? I simply do not think any of us has given a satisfactory answer to either of those questions.

Further Thoughts on Perception

It is now trite commentary to say that even the perceptible world cannot be described save through the language of experience of the perceiver, and in so far as we use a common language, we are able to communicate our experiences to a degree. I and my fellow observer can both be said to perceive the colour 'red'. But neither of us is capable of stating what it is we perceive, or describing the perception in such a way as to enable us to ascertain whether we have perceived one and the same thing. That which I perceive of as 'red' may not be, and very possibly is not, that which my fellow observer perceives as 'red'. And yet, it may well be precisely the same perception we both have. The difficulty lies not in conceiving of circumstances in which the two observers have precisely the same perception, but in being able to ascertain whether that perception, or those perceptions, are precisely the same, or even substantially similar. Though we are unable to verify whether the 'red' which I perceive is the 'red' which you perceive, it is possible to verify whether each of us perceives something to be 'red'. A simple experiment would consist of my placing a 'red' object before an observer, and then asking him or her to state its colour, repeating that several times with different observers. If each such observer calls that object 'red', then we at least can say that that object is indeed 'red', but what we cannot verify is whether 'red' as perceived by any one observer has the same properties as that perceived by another.

We have learned how to name something (for example, with the use of the word 'red'), but we are unable to describe this in such a way that multiple observers can decide whether they have each seen the same thing. To that extent, verbal communication, in particular where this concerns sensory perception, is a blunt tool which can bring us only a certain distance towards a like understanding.

Indeed, ironically, it is probably easier to try to ascertain whether two or more people share the same or very similar perceptions if one is thinking instead of abstract phenomena such as number, rather than of sensory perception, such as shape (albeit that we can also understand shape as abstract phenomena) and colour.

In conclusion, what does not appear to be capable of proof, as it were, is whether what one sees is the same or different from what someone else sees; but what *does* appear to be capable of some degree of confirmation, is the logical structure of the language we use to describe that which we can see, or the nexus between the language and the perceived world. Both observers may claim to see 'red ball', because they each know what it is for something to be 'red' and a 'ball'. What we cannot demonstrate is whether the objects these words represent 'look' the same to each of us. The ability to communicate is dependent on the recognition of the appropriate linguistic response to any given perceived phenomenon.

On a Less Than Scientific Subject Matter

Is a state of mind any different from a state of emotion? Neither is a more accurate description of the state than the other. We are moved by something, and that is the state itself, let us call it *emotio*. To the extent that we are unmoved, albeit in some conscious state of mind, the quality of *emotio* is lacking. That is all very well, and begs the question as to what such movement must comprise. Is it as if some matters of which we are aware move us, and yet other matters leave us unmoved? If we are moved, then we are in a state of emotion, but to the extent that we are conscious but remain unmoved, we are in a state of mind.

Clearly the distinction is an artificial one, and in trying to describe each state, or to distinguish between them, the language which one has at hand is of limited assistance.

Add to that the language of perception, for it does not seem credible that one can be either in a state of mind or in a state of emotion (if indeed the two are distinguishable) in the absence of the perception of something, albeit a remembered perception – a recollection.

It is said that for some of us, the processes of our minds

are so closely intertwined with the processes of our states of emotion, that the one is indistinguishable from the other. So be it.

I suggest that further than that, none of us is capable of distinguishing a state of mind or a state of emotion (both of which are much the same in terms of states) from a perception. Take, for example, an abstract thought process. And what is 'an abstract thought process' but an attempt to encapsulate a perception by way of a linguistic medium? It is said that to the Greek philosopher Plato, the beauty of things is a clue to the transcendent, and that to the older Kant, human morality plays such a part. In both cases, therefore, a perception, be it the perception or a sense of beauty (probably little more than a blend of form and shade, for one could hardly say that there is beauty in a formless monochrome, save perhaps for the somewhat 'emotive' colours black or white) or a perception of some moral precept, take for example generosity, is the necessary precursor to more abstract thought – or in short, an attempt to 'make sense' or to 'develop' such perceptions, as best one can (given the constraints of language), into more than the perception per se.

Surely, however, neither the beauty of things nor even our sense of morality is an indubitable sign that there is anything more than that. What appears to have led thinkers such as Plato or Kant to an apparently inevitable conclusion was merely the processes of thought which for each of them was a great gift and if we speak in terms of 'gift', there is a temptation to feel that that 'gift' was truly a *gift*, and if indeed it was a gift then there must be a giver thereof. To conclude that if there is such a thing as beauty (in reality, it might be closer to the truth to say that we *perceive* beauty) – to say, instead, that beauty *exists*, as we assume that a stone exists, is harder to maintain. That one may argue that a stone is beautiful, just as it is also grey and round, is also harder to maintain, simply because, as the truism goes, although we may have substantial agreement with regard to the colour 'grey' or the shape 'round', and indeed these features in our perceptions can be 'taught' and 'learned'; it is harder to imagine a situation where beauty can be learned or taught. Yes, to conclude that if there is such a thing as beauty, or such a sense as the moral sense, that that is a sign that something beautiful or something moral must exist, or otherwise, that the logical or linguistic consequence of that is that something of beauty and goodness must exist, is hard to maintain, except as an exercise in either poetry or logic. To take the argument a step further, be it through the medium of poetics or of linguistics, and argue that if there is beauty, or if there is goodness, that that must mean that there must exist something which is its ultimate form, is impossible to maintain, save as an intellectual exercise.

I am not even sure that we can maintain that argument as an exercise in logic. Would it not be like arguing that if we perceive something to exist, that something better than that must also exist, and not merely something better than that, but rather, a superlative form of that something? How does that make logical sense? The error lies in giving a quality, or a qualitative judgement (for example beauty, or the sense that something is beautiful) phenomenal form.

Inevitably, therefore, our only argument for the

existence of that which we cannot and do not ordinarily perceive is that we sense something 'other' than that which we merely perceive, and also that we sense the failure of our lives, and their invariably unwholesome nature, and it is just conceivable that when we ponder on that sensation, which we have only sometimes (oh so infrequently that that too is the very reason why our lives are so very poor), and the unwholesomeness of almost everything else we perceive, that we need, we truly need, a good father, an immaculate mother, a saving deity, somewhere, even though in a realm other than that of our perceptions (and that is really all that we have).

On Justice and Injustice

Concepts such as 'just deserts', and justice itself, are in essence of a kind with the Biblical concept of 'an eye for an eye'. Viewed simply, with such metaphors as these as visual aids, justice is apparently concerned with the almost arithmetical relationship between an action, in the broadest sense of that word, and that which ought to be its consequence. Yes, ought to be, because that consequence is not the natural result of the action. If I steal your coat, there is no natural consequence to that, except that I have what was your coat, and you do not. Justice, as a concept and also as a mode of behaviour, requires us to substitute an artificial consequence in place of the benign result of my action. But my illustration begs a question: why 'steal'? If we construe the coat as 'belonging' to someone, and incapable of not belonging, and if I then deprive you, to whom the coat 'belongs', of it, I have taken something of yours which I was not 'permitted' to take. But if the coat cannot be construed to belong, in any sense of that word, then it cannot be capable of being stolen, and my dispossessing you of it does not carry any clear consequence.

On Justice and Injustice

Another example: you have caused me an injury, and that in itself has a potentially broad definition. If that injury was undeserved, unprovoked and uninvited by me, as with the theft of the coat, you will have made an incursion on my private self. But there is no natural consequence of your having injured me; you have injured me, and that is the end of it. Without resort to the use of words such as desert, or right (as in human right), I construe of justice in such a way that the injury you have caused me ought not to have been inflicted, and I will remain dissatisfied and unappeased, unless some near equivalent harm comes to you. Putting it bluntly, as I have here, the concept of justice seems thoroughly primitive, with the sole aim of facilitating the preservation of the self. But not even that; where preservation cannot possibly be the motivation, the only apparent motivation must be the desire for revenge.

That is a legalistic view of the concept of justice. A broader definition can also be given to the word. We say that it is unjust that the world has such large numbers of poor, or that the weak are oppressed, or that there are many who do not have the benefit of employment, or the benefit of personal wealth, or the benefit of an education. We value these things and we pity those among us who have no access to one or more of them. It is not easy to construe such inequalities among us in terms of justice or injustice, because there does not appear to be a clear aggressor and a clear victim in such cases as these. We might argue that society is the aggressor, or less directly, that the powerful or the wealthy is the aggressor, and perhaps one would be correct to do so; but we have begun to lose sight of the otherwise clearly defined roles of aggressor and victim. If I am a person of substantial power and wealth, how am I responsible for the misery of the dispossessed, except in a very indirect way? That is to say I could with my substantial power and wealth alleviate that misery, and perhaps that is what I should do, but is that what we refer to when we speak of justice or injustice?

It might be said that if justice is to have a meaning in this cruel and largely indifferent world, then every poor and dispossessed soul, every hungry child, every broken spirit, is an injustice which can only be healed by uncompromising charity. What might that mean? Perhaps, that none of us deserves to have any more than any other. Perhaps the message to us all in this instance is that as long as there remains just one suffering soul among us, we do not deserve that which we have. That said, men of great ostensible faith, men of God, frequently stint on that most fundamental of beliefs and permit or condone revelry and excess among themselves, while condemning the world for having its poor. Indeed, it must be easier for a camel to enter through the eye of a needle than for a rich man to enter through the gates of heaven! Here too, our reasoning is flawed and inconsistent. Instead of condemning the rich and the powerful, and adorning ourselves with the ashes of poverty and humility, without double-mindedness, we espouse poverty and modesty but praise its opposites – even the so-called man of god is at least potentially a sycophant! If we are of the belief that we cannot worship both God and mammon at once, then let us be sure that our actions and our words, and even, for that matter, our thoughts, reflect that belief. Undoubtedly, it is a difficult belief to own, and harder still to espouse and to live accordingly. But if that is what we believe, and that is what we teach others to believe, there is surely no room for compromise.

And yet, what is the logic or the premise of that belief? Is it that wealth in reality is unequally distributed, and therefore the possession of wealth is an instance of injustice on a human scale? In which event, let us redistribute our wealth and thereby guarantee our seat in heaven! Is it that the possession of wealth is *per se* contrary to the good? In which event, notwithstanding a redistribution, for as long as we possess great wealth, which is akin to the worship of wealth, the gates of heaven are likely to be barred to us!

I have heard it said that we must be 'in the world', but not 'of the world'. That also is meaningless as a guide to our conduct, if being in the world permits us to be stronger or better endowed than others. Am I to say that I am in the world, but not of the world, if I am a man of substantial wealth living among the poor, because in spite of my wealth I remain 'unattached' to my wealth? 'Unattached' in what sense? Independent of my wealth? And if I lost everything that I own, would that please me? Would I even remain indifferent to my loss? Then why would I need that wealth at all? Let me then rid myself of all my wealth; let me pass it on as an inheritance not to one of the same kin as me, but instead to a stranger. Would that please me? To my mind, that is nothing short of a rhetorical question, because the answer cannot possibly be in the affirmative. Accordingly, to be in this world, albeit not of it, cannot mean that one can live a life of excess, by which we mean that we have something more than that possessed by many others.

But are we justified in possessing anything at all? Surely the answer should be that we are not, for as long as my neighbour is wanting in any way. So the question remains whether these teachings are the teachings merely of redistribution, or of the surrender of something inherently bad, or at the least, of something which stands in the way of the good?

I have also heard it said that men and women are the mere victims of a malicious or malignant being, or a malicious or a malignant entity; though, it appears from the nature of these thoughts, that that being must have human form, at least in as far as it appears to display qualities of mind, and qualities of will which are characteristically human – and to that extent, these thoughts are not unique. But what I find curious in these thoughts is that the underlying metaphysical structure is *sans* the concept of a benevolent being or entity, albeit one which appears to work side by side, or co-habit with, the malevolent. And it must follow from this that the experiences of the person whose views these are must be devoid of the existence of anything 'good'. For if that person were to admit the existence (in his or her experience) of even some 'good' (whatever that might be, and however defined), then this metaphysical structure fails. If one were to conclude that that which hurts us is caused, outside our own efforts, by a malevolent being, then one would have to ask oneself also whether that which gives us pleasure (let us say that which is 'good' in some sense) is likewise caused by the same malevolent being, and if so, why a malevolent being should also be munificent, or whether such pleasure is wholly without cause, and if so, why one should suppose that that which hurts us has such a cause, but yet that which brings us pleasure does not.

On the contrary, if we felt obliged to acknowledge the existence of the 'good' (in whatever form), and concluded (for some reason) that that 'good' had a cause beyond our control, then we might suppose that that cause had its origin in a benevolent being, and that side by side with that, there existed a kind of malevolent being also – we are therefore making the same assertions as are being made by and on behalf of many of the better known religions. But suppose, instead, that we were to acknowledge the existence of both pain and pleasure in human experience, and yet that we were to draw no conclusions from that, save that these stimuli surely exist. If we supposed, instead, that neither pain nor pleasure has a cause, or more radically and significantly, that neither pain nor pleasure has a cause in a being, be it a being who toys with us or one who feels compassion for us, then the vacuum which that leaves in our metaphysical structure would surely seem intolerable.

Perhaps, then, our difficulty as beings with an apparent sense of morality is to conceive of pleasure and pain as being merely coincidental rather than central to our moral sensibilities. For if one suffers pain without reason, purpose or consequence – *sans* teleology or moral grounds, and *sans*, even malevolent purpose – then that pain is intolerable. If circumstances were such as they were merely because they were, then we would have nothing to rail against, no explanations at all, no capacity for redemption – and that would truly be intolerable. And yet, how easy it is to suppose that both pain and pleasure are just that, and nothing more. And equally so, how easy it is to suppose that my pleasure or pain is mine alone and bears no relationship or consequence with your own or anyone else's, save that you may appear to perceive my pain or my pleasure, and to some extent be capable of experiencing or 'sharing' in those sensations. But if pain and pleasure were truly nothing more than coincidental to our sense of purpose, rather than central to this, then what could we make of their existence? If I suffer pain not because of its cathartic force, not because of the 'actions' of a malevolent being, and not in order to share in the greater pain of humanity or somesuch, then how intolerable my pain is!

And yet, at its simplest, I can assert that that pain is not without purpose, for it enables me to distinguish between that which can destroy me and that which causes me to thrive. Having experienced pain, I soon grow conscious of its unsavoury nature; and having experienced pleasure, I crave for more of the same. But whether one person's pain has meaning, so to speak, whether for himself or for some greater unit than that, is conceivable only in the light of a questionable teleology or a system of ethics. And perhaps it is our attempt to make system and sense of an essentially chaotic and meaningless collection of sensations that is our undoing.

But worse still, is the folly of inconsistency and haphazard reasoning...

Appendix

Footnote 5

'It is raining. I am standing in the rain. Therefore I am wet'. This does not appear to be causally correct. Rather, we should say: 'There is water on my skin. Therefore my skin is wet'. But that merely says (converting to symbolical form) A = A (or B). In short, 'My skin is covered with water; my skin is wet', or 'My skin is covered with water [wet]; [therefore] my skin is wet [covered with water]'. This is nothing short of a tautology. So, we return to the 'act of causation': 'The rain [I am standing in], has caused me to be[come] wet'. Perhaps this is better, or at least equally satisfactorily, described as follows:

1. I am standing in the rain
2. rain comprises water
3. water has the property 'wetness'
4. the rain covers my exposed skin
5. [therefore], I am wet

Alternatively:

1. my skin is covered by [wetness]
2. [therefore] I am wet[ness]

Or:

'I am wet; [therefore] I am wet'.

And now a more typical example of a causal relationship: 'smoking causes cancer'. Can this be described in the same way as I have described the example above? Possibly as follows:

1. cigarettes contain X, a carcinogen
2. a carcinogen is a substance which is found in individuals who have cancer
3. X is found to be present in individual Y's body cells
4. Y has cancer A
5. [therefore] cancer A has been caused by X

Put differently (where Y = a body; W = a chemical substance; X = cancerous cells; and controversially, A = 'associated with cancer'):

1. Y has [or contains] W
2. W is A
3. Y has X
4. [therefore W has caused X]

There are two possible assumptions here. Firstly, A itself is an assumption (namely, that the presence of a particular chemical in the body is 'cancer-associated'. Secondly, step 4 above is an assumption, rather than a genuine 'conclusion' as it seems to be.

The sequence 1 to 4, above, appears to be capable of substitution as follows:

1. Y contains W
2. Y contains X

The unnecessary steps are [If X is present, so too is W] and [therefore W has caused X]. It is almost as though we are saying: [where W is assumed to be a [sufficient] component of cancer X], Y contains X, [therefore] if Y contains W, Y will have X.

In my earlier example, 'rain', 'water' and 'wet[ness]' were roughly equivalent to one another, as used. In my later example, are we able to say that W and X are also equivalent?

If W is defined as a chemical found in a cancerous organism (or rather, tissue), possibly not yet. If we say W is a carcinogen, we may be closer to drawing that 'equivalence'. But we will need to take a number of interim steps to conclude that W *causes* X, as follows:

Appendix

1. W is a substance which we think is a carcinogen [that itself assumes 'causes cancer']
2. Y has cancer X
3. [therefore, and this is a further assumption] W has caused cancer X in Y